Tom Kundig
Working Title

Tom Kundig
Working Title

Princeton Architectural Press, New York

Contents

Foreword

Mark Rozzo

One August night several years ago, Tom Kundig and I were motoring
along Interstate 80, eastbound across the flat basin of Utah. I-80 is one
of the continent's great straightaways, connecting New York City and
San Francisco. It's about 2,900 miles (4,667 kilometers) of continuous
multilane blacktop, and it's said to be among the handful of human-made
structures visible from orbiting craft. At some point between the Bonneville
Salt Flats and Salt Lake City, an otherworldly amber glow off in the dis-
tance caught Kundig's eye. It revealed the ghostly, vaguely menacing
outlines of buildings and machinery: perhaps a mining operation or a
waste-disposal facility, outfitted with the requisite industrial gas flare that
looked like an orphaned Olympic torch. "Wow, look at that," Kundig said,
captivated by the *Mad Max*ian sight unfolding in the desert darkness.

As a landscape-attuned architect who earned his undergraduate
degree from the University of Washington in environmental design, Kundig
is no great fan of such industries per se. They have a habit of chewing
up and spitting out some of the very ecologies that have inspired his finest
work. But Kundig does have a soft spot for the built vernacular, particularly that of the American West, and he can discourse on the subject with
a mixture of scholarly precision and schoolboy wonder. "Growing up in
Spokane in the 1950s and '60s," he once told me, "it was all mining, lumber,
agriculture. I just *liked* those devices, and a lot of them are now gone. It's
a different place." (The young Kundig briefly worked in a lumber mill.)
Here then, off I-80, was a fearsome survivor of the industrial Pleistocene
that Kundig was talking about, a living fossil no doubt devouring fossil fuel
and/or delivering some form of it. It provoked a moment of fascination
and reflection for the architect. "Sawmills, mines, extraction industries,"
Kundig said. "Those things are very much a part of me, and so rooted in
this landscape."

When considering Kundig's buildings, twenty-nine examples of which
are included here in his fourth book, one is struck by how palpably they
express, and how cannily they frame, the relationship between design and
environment. Each project reminds us how complex—beautiful, thorny,
open to constant reinvention and reinvestigation—that relationship is.
In "Anecdote of the Jar" the American poet Wallace Stevens's narrator

Martin's Lane Winery
Kelowna, British Columbia,
2016

recounts the act of placing an empty jar upon a hill in Tennessee. The seemingly insignificant gesture vibrates with ontological consequence, cosmic import. Of the jar, Stevens writes, "The wilderness rose up to it, / And sprawled around, no longer wild." The lesson is that human intervention, no matter how slight, alters everything.

Like Stevens's jar, and even like those glowing industrial operations off I-80, Kundig's own structures are luminous presences within the landscape, whether they be Lilliputian fishing or writing huts, substantial houses in the wilderness or big city, or commercial projects that afford surprising intimacy at institutional scale. Obviously, Kundig's work, which has brought him a raft of laurels (along with opportunities to design in settings far-flung from his Seattle base at the firm Olson Kundig), is as removed from these infernal industries as you can imagine. His buildings get their glow not from gas flares or (God forbid) uranium caches, but

above:
Costa Rica Treehouse
Santa Teresa, Costa Rica, 2017

opposite:
River House
Ketchum, Idaho, 2017

from their ingenuity, precision, and frank materiality, turned out, as they often are, in concrete the color of moon dust and untreated steel as richly patinated as any Richard Serra sculpture. Brute strength and tactile refinement are held in precise equilibrium. As an Alpine skier and climber, Kundig knows something about risk taking, endurance, and execution.

"Tough, light, and solid," is how he once described a project to me. That triad of no-nonsense adjectives is perhaps the best description there is of Kundig architecture, which manages to combine the airy tautness of the Case Study Houses with the elemental, expressive heft you might associate with Louis Kahn. Kundig's roots—thanks in part to his father, the Swiss-born architect Moritz Kundig—run deep in the European modernist tradition. Yet his outlook is all-American, in the best sense: generous, forward-looking, inspired by the land, always in motion.

The nocturnal drive across I-80 followed a long, and very hot, day taking in the annual eardrum-challenging ritual known as Speed Week, in which homegrown vehicles blast across the Bonneville Salt Flats at speeds (and noise levels) that could rival a DC-10. Kundig has been a spectator for years, drawn to Bonneville's intersection of true American subculture and alien topography. The hot-rod culture of the 1960s (the airbrushed, souped-up creations of Ed "Big Daddy" Roth and his ilk) is another strand of Kundig's complex architectural DNA. "It's about reinventing commodities for your own purpose, in your own voice," he explained. (Kundig's residence in Seattle, where he lives with his wife, Jeannie, is known as Hot Rod House.)

The commodities Kundig reinvents in his buiidings—steel, plywood, glass, concrete—are handled with sculptural finesse. Starting at age twelve, Kundig apprenticed with the sculptor Harold Balazs, a man he calls his mentor. (Balazs's motto, which could serve as the architect's own, was "Transcend the Bullshit.") Yet Kundig, who loved drawing cars as a kid and keeps a Ducati in the garage, has always had a thing for motion and the kind of gee-whiz feats of engineering you find at Speed Week. His famous "gizmos" move multiton steel doors, shutters, and walls with the turn of a hand wheel. They bring a level of hands-on participation, along with hot-rodesque invention, that is rare in architecture.

Executing them with "gizmologist" Phil Turner, Kundig is rigorous about their application and ever vigilant lest a client request one for gratuitous reasons. At a 2008 event at the White House, where Kundig was honored for his National Design Award in architecture, I suggested that he gin up a gizmo to open the entire 170-foot (52-meter) north facade of America's best-known residence. The idea of a blast of fresh air in the executive mansion had its obvious civic appeal—not at all gratuitous, really. Kundig laughed it off, but if anyone could tackle such a challenge, it's him. The delight created by these ingenious touches has been widely, and rightly, noted. But they are also serious investigative tools. Not only do Kundig's gizmos open houses to the great outdoors, they open explorations into craft and finish, physics and hydraulics, humans and their dwellings—all while giving tactile pleasure, performing crucial functions,

opposite, above:
Burke Museum of Natural History and Culture
Seattle, Washington, 2019

opposite, below:
Shinsegae International
Seoul, South Korea, 2015

and looking cool. They also underscore the fact that Kundig architecture embodies Le Corbusier's familiar definition of a house as "a machine for living in."

Kundig creates some of those machines—whether for living or working in—from found architectural objects, convinced that skillful repurposing is a more responsible (and exciting) building strategy than even the LEEDiest prefab. Take, for instance, the Lab in Seattle, a faceless former industrial laser laboratory that Kundig transformed into an elegant art space that hosts a blue-chip private collection of Donald Judds and Dan Flavins, Anselm Kiefers and Gerhard Richters, and serves as a venue for public events. Walking through it, he marvels at the cracks spreading across the concrete floor like a system of tributaries and rivers—subtle, serendipitous patterns that could never have been cooked up on a sketch pad. (Kundig continues to shun the use of digital tools in his design process.) His award-winning Charles Smith Wines Jet City project performed architectural CPR upon a moribund Dr. Pepper bottling plant adjacent to Seattle's Boeing Field. The circa 1960s structure, formerly clad in stucco and studded with tiny windows, has become graceful and welcoming, a place to have a glass of Washington State Riesling or see a performance by the likes of Jerry Lee Lewis or watch the planes touching down across the road.

These projects are not what comes to mind when most people think of Kundig's work. People tend to think of such contemporary icons as the Chicken Point Cabin, Delta Shelter, and Slaughterhouse Beach House— projects that have made Kundig one of the most revered designers of residential space in the world. But for him, an artful intervention upon an existing structure provides an important lesson that fuels an increasingly significant aspect of his practice. "Buildings are inherently beautiful, even if they're ugly," he told me, bringing to mind that baleful operation we saw on I-80. "In fact, when someone says, 'It's ugly,' I get even more excited."

Kundig likes to build on ecotones, topographical boundary lines where two types of landscape or flora collide: forest and grassland, say, or land and water. It requires a daredevil spirit to build in these zones, along with deep insight into the natural world. The fascination with ugliness and beauty

is one of the many ecotones that run through Kundig's work—along with
the lines between art and craft, refinement and elementalism, toughness
and softness, inside and outside, futurism and timelessness, solidity and
motion, transcendent form and earthy materiality, and, always, architecture
and landscape.

This year is the nineteenth since Kundig became an owner of his firm,
which employs 190 persons in a thrumming three-story headquarters
in Seattle's Pioneer Square. As he bounds up and down the office's open
staircase or gets ready for dash out to Sea-Tac for a flight taking him to
a new project in Sun Valley, Idaho, or Seoul, he radiates relentless move-
ment and groundedness in equal measure. This is Tom Kundig's personal

University of Washington Department of Architecture Distinguished Alumni Award Acceptance Speech

Tom Kundig, FAIA, RIBA
April 6, 2019

Thank you all for this deep honor. As wonderful as honors based on rec[ent] work are, I think honors based on an extended career are the most mea[n]ingful. As a side note, I've also wondered if the current popular project awa[rd] programs—which are always time limited to recent work—might be rec[on]sidered to evaluate only projects that are at least ten years old. That wo[uld] be a game changer. At its root, architecture is a long story. I do believe [t]ruly important architecture becomes more meaningful with time.

The question for me today is: How do you summarize an education[al] [e]xperience from forty-five years ago succinctly and smartly in a few mi[nu]tes? It's impossible, really. Best to keep the points short and quick, to a [c]ouple of highlights out of many that continue to affect my current care[er.]

The first point was something that happened in literally the first fi[ve] [m]inutes of my first day of studio at the University of Washington Scho[ol] [A]rchitecture. I believe all of us in that studio experienced a career realit[y] [m]oment that day. Professor Philip Thiel emerged from his office adjacer[t] [t]o the studio, stopped about halfway through the door, scanned the roo[m] [a]nd in a profoundly intimidating voice asked loudly, "Did you all consciou[sly] [v]olunteer to take this studio? Do you understand your decision? You sti[ll] [h]ave time to reconsider." He went on to say, "You are going to work you[r] [a]sses off over the next sixteen weeks. Your professors have an impossib[le] [t]ask. You are completely unprepared to be architects, and it is ridiculou[s] [t]o assume in a few years that somehow you will miraculously become o[ne.] [W]e have to start that work in earnest—it's already too late."

We collectively sat there in stunned silence. He went on to suggest [t]hat we would not be architects after graduation and that some of us [w]ould never be architects—that it was up to us, and us alone. It's impos[sib]le to describe fully Phil's sixteen-week course. Together, we fumbled [t]hrough a humbling but powerful series of crazy-difficult weekly sketch tests. Seemingly, those sketch problems had nothing to do with architecture. However, I know now they were a deep root that had everything to do with architecture.

One can only experience this kind of moment in an academic setting. The most important kernel of truth in that first five minutes was the impossible task of training to be an architect in that short a period of time. Some of us came from backgrounds that might imply some sort of head start—the arrogance of youth in every generation. Phil implied that we would know very little about architecture when we graduated. And he was right. My training continues today, and I can say that UW was a critical basis point for the next many years.

I can also say after forty years that Phil Thiel was spot-on about the difficulty of becoming an architect. It takes time, experiences, and deep commitment to reach architecture's potential. I was recently asked what makes truly meaningful architecture: an architecture that works at all levels and stands the test of time. I reflected on my own career to answer this: Why were some of my projects stronger than others? What was missing or lacking in the less successful ones? I finally concluded that for the most part, it's true that architects (including students) can solve a problem with an appropriate big idea or diagram—a big move. But where the real departures begin to be understood, when experiencing the truly great projects of Louis Kahn, Carlo Scarpa, Peter Zumthor, Glenn Murcutt, Le Corbusier, Álvaro Siza, and many others, is that they succeed at the nuance level.

They not only solve the larger problems of the parti and deliver the bigger, more flamboyant moves but also comprehend the underground soul of the project—the heart—through complete understanding that transcends style. The overtones and undertones of subtly silent proportions, fit and finish, and graceful flow that can be developed only with time and study. They succeed at the second or third look. The nuance is at the nano level, the quiet level, the human level.

And that, I believe, was Thiel's point. This is not shaking-it-out-of-your-sleeve parti stuff, the Pinterest or Instagram moment—it is about the level beneath the first impressions, like a book or poem that one reads over and

again that gets better with each reading. Not unlike the music of Miles Davis, Jimi Hendrix, or Ludwig van Beethoven. The more you listen, the richer your understanding becomes. The best projects get better with time, and that next level of richness is found in an underlying degree of nuance.

I've always made a point of identifying those critical professors for me at the UW School of Architecture: Phil Thiel, Hermann Pundt, Astra Zarina, Steven Holl, Grant Hildebrand, John Rohrer, Doug Zuberbuhler, Omer Mithun, Wendell Lovett, Victor Steinbrueck, Richard Haag, Larry Rouch, Tom Kubota. There is no question I'm missing some. But wow—what I've learned as I enter the fourth quarter of my career is that academic training is only the first critical step in the practice of architecture. The colleagues, friends, clients, and makers I work with continue to astound me with their untitled roles as professors, gurus, and teachers. Fifty years ago our office

Tom Kundig at the Olson Kundig
office, Seattle, Washington

was founded by—and impossible to thank enough—fellow UW graduate Jim Olson. Thirty years ago our office was 7 people. Today we are 190, with a crazy-fantastic portfolio of projects that spans the world. What a wonderful adventure of working our asses off—fumbling at times but always focused on producing good work and leaving the world a better place. And in retrospect, I could not have been luckier to have met and been taught by the collection of characters at the UW School of Architecture.

I've also come to understand fully that the architecture we are privileged to engage in is really just a final physical manifestation of the context in which we live. An idiosyncratic moment of place and people. If a building moves, it doesn't move far. Architecture at its best is a thoughtful reflection of the context of time, place, and culture.

This brings me to my final thought in considering possible next steps for my career. I can circle back to Phil Thiel and his sketch problems of forty-five years ago. One of his assignments continues to haunt me today: a seemingly simple problem that carried a subversive message. This sketch problem started as a study to design an "algorithm of chaos" that would randomly fill in a grid of squares in some unknown, chaotic pattern, using dice as the chaos element to either fill squares, leave empty squares, or strike diagonal patterns of empty or full with all four points of the square as options. To fill in the grid per our algorithm, we were each asked to pick what Phil described as "the two ugliest colors in the world." Easy enough. We all picked our colors. In short order, looking at the colors our colleagues picked as ugly, we were surprised and didn't necessarily agree with their choices. In fact, some of the ugly colors others picked were quite beautiful, I thought.

We continued with the sketch problem and our ugly colors, each filling in our grid of squares with our own algorithm of chaotic decisions. When we finished, Phil asked us all what we thought. We collectively realized our grids were each quite beautiful and almost reluctantly agreed that our own ugly colors were, in fact, not all that ugly. Phil's point with the subversive sketch problem was that there are no ugly colors, only colors used inappropriately. To say something was ugly was missing a potential that could be the difference between ordinary and extraordinary. Fantastic.

A Conversation between Tom Kundig and Michael Chaiken

When I was asked to interview Tom Kundig for this, his fourth book, I was a little taken aback. I first met him in 2017, shortly after the George Kaiser Family Foundation brought the Bob Dylan Archive to Tulsa, Oklahoma. At the time, I was working as a freelance archivist in New York, assisting filmmakers, writers, and, recently with Dylan, a musician in organizing their archives. Tom and I share a mutual friend, the owner of Pierre Chareau's Maison de Verre in Paris. Beyond that, my connection to the world of architecture is, at best, negligible. The editors reassured me that Tom wasn't particularly interested in talking with another professional in the field. He was as curious about my work as I was about his.

The more I got to know Tom, whose architectural firm, Olson Kundig, won an international competition to build the Bob Dylan Center, which will be the public face of the archive, the more I came to appreciate his curious, existential mind. He's an inquisitive skeptic for whom the world is always out there to be discovered. I had the privilege of spending two days with him, making site visits to many of the buildings featured in this book. My time with him not only furthered my understanding of his work but also deepened my insight into the role architecture plays in people's lives. The conversation from our final afternoon together is recorded here.

Michael Chaiken
Curator, Bob Dylan Archive

February 28, 2019
Seattle, Washington

Michael Chaiken   I'd seen the photographs in this book, but after visiting, I appreciate how organic these buildings are.

Tom Kundig   I'm glad to hear that. Ultimately, architecture is experiential. It's like music. Sure, you can listen to a digital recording or a superb analog recording, but live? That's a whole different kettle of fish. Architecture is all about experience. Because it's a back-of-the-head experience. If you're looking at a photograph, it's a reminder, a reflection. It's front-of-the-head and not felt by all the senses.

MC   As I was going around Seattle with you, I kept thinking, "What's the husk here? What's the thing unifying all of these projects?" There are the poetic, personal flourishes in all of the buildings we visited, but the thing that struck me is that you aren't particularly dogmatic in your approach. You don't have an a priori style. What determines the architecture is the people involved, the building site, the landscape that you're working against. I say *against* because there always seems to be this creative struggle between the given and the indeterminate.

TK   That's exactly it. Or, to your point, there might be some DNA that connects them all, but ultimately, they're forged by factors that are unique to each project. As far as not being particularly dogmatic, I grew up in a somewhat socialist populist environment where if an artist were asked by an academic, "What does art mean?" they would likely answer, "It means food for my family." I remember seeing a quote that some artist wrote on his barn that said, "The believers sing the songs, the zealots pick the songs." That resonated with me. I was just remarkably uninterested in doing the same thing or having the same processes lead to the same conclusions.

Husk is a great term because it bundles all of these ideas together. In some ways, I have no idea how it all works, but if I think about my life and the things that I've always been interested in, what ties it together is the idea of going out and having some sort of an adventure. I don't mean like a death-defying adventure. It has much more to do with being sixty-four years old, still thinking about what's going on and not knowing the answers. And being fine with not knowing the answers. I'm on this planet for a short period, so I need to keep moving and try not to waste time.

My mentors have all worked their asses off, but what constitutes their work is really just a series of explorations fueled by curiosity.

    I have a real appreciation for people like physicist Richard Feynman, whose entire method of inquiry follows that premise. He just wanted to know how things worked. Well, why does that screw cap work? What's really going on with the forces in that thing? And can I describe why a screw cap is such a fascinating simple machine? It's one of the seven simple machines. It's an unbelievable thing, but most people don't even think about it. Feynman thought about it, and I do too.

MC   On your recommendation, I watched some of Feynman's lectures and interviews. He's someone who doesn't seem to lapse into despair or cynicism when confronted with the limits of our understanding of the universe. For him, answers beget more questions. He's happiest, it seems, when confronted with unanswerable questions.

K   I think that's absolutely true. He often implies that the most joyful moments for him are when he doesn't understand something.

MC   Which is a tough way for most of us to exist, I think, because it allows for a fair amount of uncertainty and chaos to creep into our lives. There's nothing more difficult than living with painful, unanswerable paradoxes.

K   For sure. Like Feynman says, God may be the answer, but I don't know. And because I don't know, I'm not going to accept the fact that there is a God. He said, "Well, maybe it is true." But that's an uncomfortable situation. And yet, that's part of what drives him. And on some level, it's what drives me too. That omnivorous quest for knowledge. Maybe that's the husk you're looking for. The magazines on the side of my bed are not architecture magazines. I'm not at all interested in architecture magazines. I'm more interested in simple, less specialized reading like the *Smithsonian* or *National Geographic*. What I don't do particularly well is auger into the subjects I'm interested in. It's almost like if you dig too deeply, all of a sudden you're not keeping your eye on other things that are happening, whether it's popular culture or current events. I'm not an expert on the current music scene, but I'm certainly interested in it. I'm not an expert on movies, but I'm interested in them too. My sense is that a similar trajectory led you to the Dylan Archive.

MC My case is a little different, but maybe having capacious interests is a way of reacting against the notion of "the expert" or "the professional." Experts are eventually burdened by the upkeep of their own expertise. When that happens, it becomes harder for new ideas to get through. I don't see myself as an expert on Dylan. Likewise, I don't see myself as any kind of artist. To my mind, being an artist involves more risk than my lower-middle-class background would ever allow for. I read widely into all kinds of things and developed skills that eventually introduced me to the artists I most admired. People like filmmakers Albert Maysles and D. A. Pennebaker, the writer Norman Mailer, all of whom I've been lucky enough to have worked with. Archiving wasn't something I went to school for— I learned what I needed to know through a lot of luck and happenstance. That said, I aggressively made my own breaks by presenting myself to people like Mailer and offering them help. I'm grateful they were receptive to it and didn't perceive me as some kind of dilettante. One project led to another. My background is largely in film and curating film programs. I did that for a number of years. There's this great line in Jean-Luc Godard's *Masculin-Féminin* (1966). One of the characters says to Jean-Pierre Léaud, "You know, moles are blind, but they dig in a certain direction." That stuck with me. It rings true. Or true in my case. I have a deep, nearly Talmudic, interest in different areas of culture, but I couldn't tell you what it all adds up to or where I'm going with it. A combination of earnestness, hard work, and a basic need to support myself led to the Dylan Archive. I wish I could say it was pure expertise.

TK I'd say the only expertise I have (if you can even call it that) is that I've got a pretty good set of tools. I can be handed a situation and, whatever that situation calls for, I can make something out of it. It's like when I used to mountain climb. The climbing gear was nothing more than a series of devices that I would somehow repurpose to get me where I was going, despite having no idea where that was. I was constantly confronted with challenges and surprises, but that's what makes the sport interesting. Overcoming resistance, creating a path.

MC I like that analogy. There's something analogous here to Dylan and his working method. Often when people write about Dylan or talk about him, they describe his career in terms of periods or breaks. His early Woody Guthrie period, his folk-rock period of the mid-1960s, the country period of the early 1970s, followed by the Christian period and on and on through the years. *Nashville Skyline* (1969) could broadly be categorized as a country record, and *Slow Train Coming* (1979) is a gospel record, but when Dylan made those career turns, he never renounced any of the things that came before. All of these moments continue to live and exist within him and, in truth, always have. "Blowin' in the Wind," Dylan's first major song, is gospel, a genre he wouldn't find his way into for another twenty years.

TK   I completely agree with that. I remember people saying that Dylan's Christian period was somehow a misstep or a misdirection. In actuality, moments like that are an important part of the journey. If we're lucky, they inform our future. When I was an angsty sixteen-year-old in Spokane, Washington, the philosophy of Alan Watts helped to settle me down a bit. I was attracted to this somewhat Buddhist notion that you are either holding on to a rock in this metaphorical river that's running around us, or you're holding on to a log and traveling along with the currents. For a kid who didn't know what the future held, Watts helped me to realize that I could become involved in things larger than myself.

        Climbing was also a big part of that. It wasn't necessarily fun, but it was an unbelievable commitment. I remember seeing this film on Swiss climber Ueli Steck. He climbed Mount Annapurna solo. No one had ever done that before, since it was considered such an insane climb. Anyway, he comes down off the mountain and says to the camera, "Nothing has changed in the world except me." That idea stayed with me. I don't think anybody, least of all myself, held out any sort of significant future for me. A guy like Dylan, of course, already had it. Almost as if he were preordained to meet his destiny head-on.

MC   I think for him, it was radio. Radio gave him a sense that there was a world bigger than his hometown of Hibbing, Minnesota.

TK   Yeah, that's interesting. For me, it was the classic American boy thing—hot rods. As a kid, I loved what was coming out of the radio, but it was car culture that really did it for me. I could give you the exact year certain cars were built the same way people can rattle off when certain records were released. I just loved what people could do with cars. Modifying them. I found it fascinating.

MC   For me, weirdly, it was *Mad* magazine. Not only did it get me reading at eight or nine, but it taught me something important about culture and satire. I especially loved old issues from the 1950s and 1960s. My parents' era. I learned about our recent past via *Mad*. Which is kind of absurd, but at the same time, it had me going to the library to find out what I could about the Beatles, the Kennedys, Richard Nixon, Chairman Mao, whoever. I obsessively read old papers and magazines, scoured flea markets for old records and books, fell in love with popular and underground culture.

The feminist author Germaine Greer once described archives as the "pay dirt of history." It's a great way to characterize them. Having worked in several, you begin to see how interconnected all this history is. The crossover of people and places. The cliché of "It's a small world" is absolutely true, especially when looking at the great cultural movements of the twentieth and early twenty-first centuries.

Anyway, by the time I was a teenager, like everyone else in the early nineties, I wanted to be a rock star. In reality, I was destined to become a dusty antiquarian. I suppose digging into all of these cultural archives, I've come to fulfill some part of my destiny. As for hot-rodding cars, I was fascinated by all of that stuff—I thought Jim Morrison's 1967 Shelby Mustang was the coolest car in the world, but growing up in Philadelphia, it wasn't any part of my reality. Were you a car tinkerer from an early age?

TK   I don't know if I was a tinkerer. I just realized that before I could really do anything, I'd need to make a commitment and learn my tools well.

MC   It's that classic line in Dylan's "A Hard Rain's A-Gonna Fall": "I'll know my song well before I start singin'." Since I don't have specialized knowledge in architecture, when looking at your work, my referents are music, painting, and film.

TK   There's a famous if overworn quote, "Architecture is frozen music."

MC   I could see that. Your work reminds me of the great color-field painters. Mark Rothko. Barnett Newman. And, of course, the sculptures of Richard Serra. How did you develop your visual sensibility? Were these guys any kind of influence?

TK   Oh, sure, but I don't think it was any one thing per se, just simply taking in as much as I could and, whether consciously or not, editing out things that didn't resonate. I watched a lot of cartoons as a kid, as well as, like I said, people building hot rods. That made a bigger impression on me than any single artist or tradition. I pull from a lot of different sources, but I know there are certain things that I can't do really well. Anything overly fancy or over-the-top, forget about it. Proportions are more import-ant to me than aesthetics, since proportions are what ultimately define how a structure looks. Why does a Ferrari feel right and a Prius doesn't? They're two very different ideas. I guess, at bottom, what concerns me most is authenticity. In any of my decisions, it's important that there's a sense of realness.

Wagner Education Center,
the Center for Wooden Boats
Seattle, Washington, 2019

MC   You mean in terms of the materials that you are using?

TK   Yes, exactly. I'll work with plastic so long as it looks like plastic and I'm not being asked to try to make it look like wood.

MC   When we were standing outside the Center for Wooden Boats, it reminded me of something very specific: the films of Jacques Tati. Do you know his work? It was almost as if I were looking at one of Tati's hypercinematic wide shots where activity is happening in every corner of the frame. The security guard sitting behind his desk, the workshop where the boats are being restored, the top floors with people milling about. All of this activity bifurcated by windows and walls, frames within frames—it gave me the impression of watching a Tati film. From a certain vantage point, you could see all of these pieces working together in madcap harmony.

TK   That's exactly it.

MC   With Tati, every inch of his frame is kinetic. There's often very little distinction between foreground and background. It's a cinematic plane where everything's equal, related, and codependent.

TK   I never really thought of it that way, but there's some truth in that. I want things to move and I want things to work. For me, Tati's *Mon Oncle* (1958) is such a great movie because it's a poke in the rib of modernism. The stuffiness of it all, particularly the way in which modernism was hijacked and turned into the monster that it's become. Tati is so funny and spot-on with his commentary. It's one of my favorite movies and not just for the inside jokes. It's the way he paces and choreographs his shots, how characters need to go downstairs to go upstairs. There's all of this layering and nuance. It's like the first time I heard Jimi Hendrix or Miles Davis. It took me a few listens before I got it, but when I did, it was a game changer.

MC   Let's talk more specifically about the projects in the book. The Burke is the first that you took me to visit. Clearly, it's a personal one.

TK   Yeah, the Burke is a really important project for my career. In so many ways, the Burke represents something that I've always aspired to, which is to understand all of the "ologies" and work through all of these scientific disciplines. I want to help demystify them. Of course, I'm not the one doing the demystification. Hopefully the curators and the collection managers will become part of that process. I sometimes say architecture is analogous to the bass line in music. It's the root note, the part that holds it all down. The Burke is a perfect example of this. I'm simply laying a foundation allowing for people to discover and explore. The architecture should serve this purpose and not get in the way, if that makes any sense.

MC   It comes across in the unfussiness of the space.

TK   That's why it's raw; that's why it's so simple. It's not flamboyant. In fact, some people might even argue that it looks a little boring, you know, that it looks a little pedestrian. It's just a big box.

MC   Your personal sensibility is evident in the wood and metalwork, but what elevates the architecture is seeing how animated the Burke becomes when people are moving through it. Also, the size of this particular frame is enormous. You can look straight through, from one side to the other. It's a

opposite:
Burke Museum of Natural History and Culture
Seattle, Washington, 2019

29

museum turned inside out. Since the conservation labs are all visible to the public, I appreciate how work is given equal billing to these incredible archaeological artifacts. When we walked in, you knew every single person there by name.

TK   Ha. Well, it's been an eleven-year project, so I better know their names!

MC   It also speaks to the collaborative nature of this project.

TK   I try to know just about everybody I work with on all of these projects, including the craftspeople. I certainly know the contractor and the superintendents. I know the clients and I know their kids. I know the administration. They become friends and cultural touchstones for the rest of your life.

MC   That's the other thing that became apparent to me about your work: all the different hats you are forced to wear. It's more than just architecture; there's this whole political side. Dealing with city ordinances, inspectors, boards of directors. I got to know the work of environmental artists Jeanne-Claude and Christo through Albert Maysles. Albert and his brother David made a series of documentary portraits on them. Jeanne-Claude and Christo shared the most intense collaborative vision. They were uncompromising and willing to move heaven and earth—sometimes literally—to see their large-scale public projects realized. I imagine you have advocates who get it almost immediately, but there's probably an equal number of people who say, "I don't see it."

TK   But I love that.

MC   It must be taxing, though.

TK   Sometimes, but it keeps the blade sharp. It forces you to try all of these different strategies, some of which you would never have thought of otherwise.

MC   We looked at a number of private homes over these past two days. My sense is that these projects give you the opportunity to play and run through riffs, since the politics aren't as intense.

TK   Private clients are completely different from public clients. The public client is usually pretty risk averse. Simply put: they do not want to take risks with other people's money. With the private clients I work with, this is their realm, and they are usually willing to go further out on a limb. I mean, the fact that they're hiring an architect already puts them in an extraordinary category. On some level, they're doing it because they actually want to engage with the process. We don't necessarily agree all of the time, but I am always very interested in understanding who they are, so I can answer what it is they're asking for. In these situations, you're essentially solving a climbing route and giving the client an end route. Along the way, I want to use these moments as places to experiment and think about other ways of using materials, technology, and structure. I think your music analogy works, because it is like sharpening your scales. You get into something, and you're not necessarily thinking about where your fingers are landing. It's back to Hendrix. He played inside and outside the blues scale to create something wholly other. Bum notes be damned. He even made those work. Which might be where the analogy with architecture ends.

MC   Right. If you measure something wrong, even by an inch, you're in trouble. But, like with Hendrix, there's an improvisatory element in what you're doing. Especially at the start and those early conceptual sketches of yours that I've seen. There are a lot of question marks written across those pages.

TK   It all has to begin somewhere. To stretch this analogy a little further, one of the lessons I've learned from Hendrix—and appreciate in Dylan— is that they aren't striving for perfection, you know? Perfection is this dangerous road to go down. Why is this unfinished steel more interesting than a perfectly painted black sheet of steel? Where some would see imperfections, I look at it as part of the tapestry that makes a building totally unique and beautiful.

MC   While we're on the subject of imperfections, I'd like to talk to you about the notion of ugly buildings. Is that even a concept you can get your head around?

TK   Funny. That's a very good question. I don't actually think there is such a thing as an ugly building. There are simply buildings that are unfortunately assembled. And deep inside, any unfortunately assembled building is a beautiful building. You just have to remove the unfortunate layers. A perfect example of this is the Dr. Pepper bottling plant that we turned into Charles Smith Wines Jet City. Everybody thought that was a dud of a building. Our attitude was, "Well, no, let's rethink it . . ."

holds true
natures of
singular,
It's interest-
lan Archive
wrote about
ad put
ays Jimi's

MC It's that armature that allows you to hot-rod it the same way Hendrix took "All Along the Watchtower" into some other dimension.

TK That's exactly right. Maybe that's why that particular piece in the archive was so meaningful to me. It's stunning in its own right while also revealing so much about Dylan's character.

MC I'm glad you think the analogy isn't too much of a stretch. People reading this might not be as forgiving.

TK No, I totally get it. It makes sense. I love those sad-sack buildings that everybody is ignoring. The ones everybody wants to tear down. We shouldn't just let these buildings rot. We'd lose all the embodied energy of our ancestors. You know, it's like somebody once said, "Every car on the road is a used car." It's now proven that the most sustainable building strategy is to repurpose an old building. It's not to tear down a bad old

Shinsegae International

Seoul, South Korea

This fifteen-story tower is the new headquarters for Shinsegae International, one of Korea's oldest and largest luxury clothiers. It unites more than five hundred Shinsegae employees, who were previously spread between several buildings throughout the city. The program includes staff offices and meeting spaces, design studios, a rooftop garden, and ground-level retail and restaurant spaces that face onto a public plaza.

The building's high-performance facade is a direct response to the client's desire for a corporate flagship that departs from the look and feel of modern commercial buildings. Designed to meet Korea's progressive energy codes, which are more rigorous than US LEED standards, the building features a gridded exoskeleton that functions as an energy performance strategy. Frit patterns on the glass reduce heat gain while optimizing thermal comfort and maximizing natural daylight year-round. Seven custom eight-foot-diameter (two-and-a-half-meter-diameter) steel wheels open and close thirty-five-foot-tall (eleven-meter-tall) external panels to modulate daylight at street level. The dynamic ethos of the fashion world is evoked by these kinetic components, which morph and change throughout the course of the day. Each time the panels are engaged, the building's presence is altered anew.

It was intentional on my part to reconsider how these tall buildings in cities are articulated. I thought the proportions of Shinsegae were beautiful, and maybe the subtlety and nuance will be appreciated in the next fifty or a hundred years, rather than if it were a one-liner in a crazy shape.

For the client, the base of this building had to be interesting not only to the people in their cars, but also to the people inside the building. They understood

The facade is intended to move like fabric does—changing positions and proportions, which is especially important at the city level of visual engagement with the building.

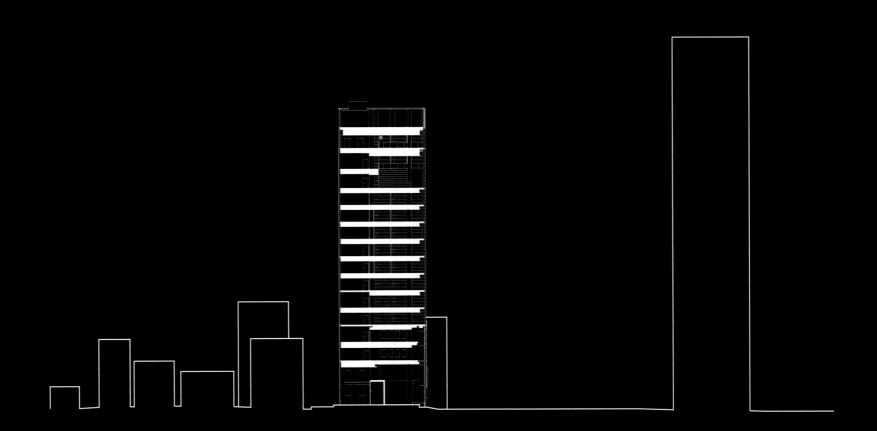

River House

Ketchum, Idaho

This compact home balances privacy and transparency, with a neighborhood road on one side and a forested riverbank on the other. The shallow sixty-foot-wide (eighteen-meter-wide) site demanded a nimble transition between these two opposing faces. The design solution was to soften the concrete and weathering steel walls of the street-facing side with punctuated moments of transparency and overhead daylighting. The other half of the home opens almost completely to the natural landscape, extending the livable space outdoors to the Big Wood River.

Several manually operated gizmos, including a corner guillotine window in the kitchen that opens to a walk-up bar, allow the owner to break down the barrier between indoors and outdoors. Dual-sided floor-to-ceiling glazing in the central interior walkway lends the sense that one is walking through the natural landscape, even inside the home.

The home transitions seamlessly from
the private side facing the road to the

The design is intended to embrace the landscape of Sun Valley as much as possible, with quite a bit of transparency facing the riverbank.

Charles Smith Wines Jet City

Seattle, Washington

Originally a Dr. Pepper bottling plant and later a recycling center, this building preserves much of its hard-won industrial patina while opening up to the surrounding Seattle neighborhood, the runways of Boeing Field, and dramatic views of Mount Rainier. On the roof, nearly seven-foot-tall (two-meter-tall) letters wrap the building in billboard fashion, announcing, "Charles Smith Wines Jet City."

The 1960s structure is composed of two elements: a two-floor office building and a contiguous steel open-truss warehouse. Together they provide space for the entire wine-making process, from grape crush to barrel storage and bottling to tasting rooms and sales. The transformation of the building involved the removal of a portion of the exterior street-side facade, replacing it with a nineteen-by-sixty-foot (six-by-eighteen-meter) span of windows, opening the interior space to the surrounding context.

Before

This project is about folding together
the unfound beauty of the building
with the larger-than-life spirit that is
Charles Smith.

West Edge Tower

Seattle, Washington

This thirty-nine-story, 440-foot-tall (134-meter-tall) mixed-use skyscraper is in Seattle's downtown core. Containing residential units, ground-level retail, and a destination Sky Bar with glass-floored observation cubes offering unobstructed views of Pike Place Market and Puget Sound, the tower graces this significant area of Seattle with respect.

The design responds to its urban setting at street level and emphasizes the expansive natural beauty unveiled above. The lower seven stories relate to the pedestrian experience and the history of early urban buildings in Seattle, which hovered around the seven-story mark. Above, the remaining thirty-two stories take on another character. Playing off the design of nearby Seattle Tower, which progresses from darker- to lighter-colored brick as it ascends, West Edge's exterior metal panels and spandrel glass transition from gray to white on the upper levels. This silvery color palette offers a subtle nod to the graduated shades of Pacific Northwest skies.

I'm most excited about how this building relates to its context—to the pedestrian experience on the lower levels, and to Seattle's natural landscape and the urban built environment above.

Meg Home

Seattle, Washington

The design of this home establishes a duality of enclosure and openness, creating a place of refuge while embracing opportunities for prospect views. The site is a dense, constricted lot in Seattle's Queen Anne neighborhood with panoramic views of downtown and Puget Sound. The design addressed the site's twenty-three-foot (seven-meter) grade change through scale: the home is smaller and more discreet on the street side, with only two visible stories, and larger in the back, where three floors are visible. A lower roof height over the entrance facade amplifies and connects these two scales. The home's main level is open and expansive, with a two-story guillotine window wall that opens via a hand-cranked wheel to a cantilevered deck and city views. This voluminous space with its barrel-vaulted ceiling contrasts with the more intimate, private areas of the home located above and below.

With Meg Home, we wanted to balance transparency with a sheltering sense of refuge. It's the yin and the yang.

The goal was to establish a play
between grittiness and finesse—
to make beauty by contrast.

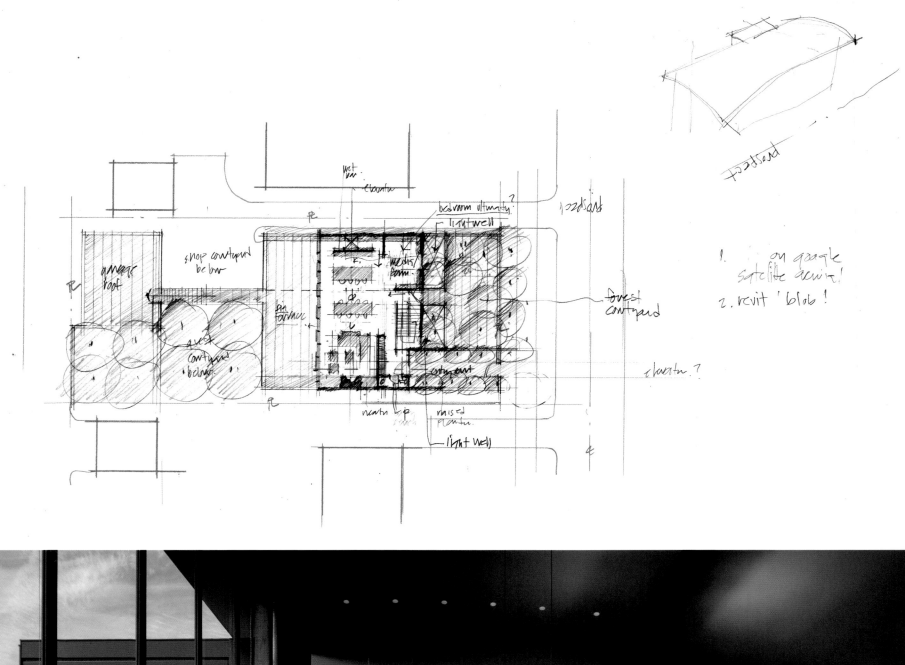

prospect

bedroom ultimately?
lightwell

shop courtyard
below

garage
roof

guest
courtyard
below

bar
terrace

medis/
bath

forest
courtyard

elevatn?

north up
porch

raised
planter

(light well)

1. ... on google
   satelite revit!

2. revit 'blob'!

MrSteam

Long Island City, New York

This headquarters for a steam shower manufacturing company embraces the industrial nature of the firm's business as well as the building itself, which MrSteam has occupied since the 1960s. A minimal, bright redesign of the interior space highlights the raw, historic character of the hardworking building. The new design links past to present, revealing the original structural elements of the 1931 building and combining them with new insertions that meet the needs of MrSteam's growing professional sales and operations staff.

Reconsidering the industrial building meant sandblasting the original concrete columns to reveal a palimpsest of original textures, materials, and historic signage. Steel brackets clamped to these columns support floating plywood partitions in the open-plan office, which affords views of Manhattan and three bridges leading there. Full-height glazing delineates peripheral offices, allowing daylight to reach the interior core's central work space. A retractable overhead bifold door connects the conference room to the adjacent showroom, allowing teams to reveal new products during client presentations. Throughout, an emphasis on clean, white walls and elemental, unfinished materials exists in a dialogue with the industrial vocabulary of the original space.

From the start, the client recognized there were some very interesting and beautiful elements in this historical manufacturing building—it just had to be reconsidered. It was exciting to unearth the possibility and potential that were lying just beneath the surface.

The industry of industry is actually quite beautiful. With the design for MrSteam, we wanted to uncover and respect the original industrial nature of the building. The hope was to reveal the underlying beauty of what industry represents, which is the engagement with and harnessing of natural forces.

and home furnishings launched in 2012—complete the industrial aesthetic.

Organized around two parallel circulation corridors, the apartment has two entrances—one opening to a vestibule with custom corner doors and the other with a custom interlocking, two-part puzzle door. Adjacent to the open living, dining, and kitchen area is a blackened-steel wall that can be raised into the ceiling via a hand-cranked wheel to reveal a red-accented bar. A swing-arm TV pivot gizmo transforms the living area from a space for intimate family gatherings to one for large game-day events. Walnut casework, dark bronze window mullions, and black terrazzo floors create an interior refuge against the exposure of the apartment's full-surround window walls.

An exciting challenge for me was bringing the tectonic spirit of my work to this sophisticated, refined residence in an urban center.

Triptych

Narrow Point, Washington

Triptych was designed for a family with a significant art collection. In this home, art is meant to be experienced on a very personal and accessible level; the family wanted its enjoyment to be intertwined with their daily lives. The design speaks to the relationship between art and life, as custom art installations and gallery spaces are interwoven with domestic spaces throughout the home, including the kitchen, living room, and dining room. Because the family hosts many gatherings and cultivation events, the building had to be both intimate and public, depending on changing needs. A flexible design allows the family to rotate their art through interior and exterior spaces as their collection grows and their artistic interests evolve. The design balances the gritty authenticity of raw materials with humanistic artworks that weave throughout the home and the landscape.

With this home, art is meant to be experienced on a very personal, intimate level. Art is interwoven with spaces for everyday family life, both inside and outside, reflecting the significant role that the arts hold for this family.

Hale Lana

Kona, Hawaii

This family retreat on Hawaii's Big Island takes the form of several pavilions dispersed around the site, linked by elevated wooden lanais and a series of gardens. The home takes a position at the ecotone line between a heavily landscaped area and expansive ocean views that stretch to Haleakalā volcano on nearby Maui.

Cantilevered double-pitched roofs in the Big Island style create deep canopies that encircle the buildings and their lanais, allowing the pavilions to open completely to ocean breezes while remaining protected from the sun. These canopies, combined with a high degree of glazing throughout, create the sense that the architecture is hovering over the landscape; the home's name, Hale Lana, translates to "floating home." Operable shutter screens let the family tune each building to changing environmental conditions, adjusting to the desired degree of sun, air, and privacy. At Hale Lana, the line between inside and outside is almost nonexistent, allowing the family to feel at one with the Hawaiian climate and landscape.

The intention was for the home to feel like a canopy on the Hawaiian landscape, transparent between inside and outside.

Hale Lana's roofs pick up on the local Hawaiian vernacular, in which large canopy roofs gather prevailing trade wind breezes and keep them moving through the building. However, this project takes that idea to a new level structurally, with a very long cantilever and an extremely precise leading roof edge.

Martin's Lane Winery

Kelowna, British Columbia

Tucked into a hillside, the design of this winery embraces the topography of the land and the gravity-flow wine-making process taking place inside. The building is conceived as a rectangular form with a central split or fracture down the middle. Its production side follows the direction of the site, utilizing the downhill slope for its gravity-flow process. The other half, containing the visitor area, cantilevers over the vineyards, offering views of nearby Okanagan Lake and the mountains beyond.

The functional areas of Martin's Lane step down the hillside, from the grape-receiving area at the top, through fermentation and the settling room, down to the bottling room on the aboveground level and finally the belowground barrel storage area. Throughout, visitor spaces are woven into the manufacturing areas, including a tasting room, a dining room, and visitor walkways that offer intimate glimpses of the production process. Much like the building itself, interior details such as a spiral steel staircase inspired by the Fibonacci sequence of grapevines tell the story of the highly refined, artisanal wine-making process of Martin's Lane.

The building is split into two parts, with one part literally following the land and the other part following the horizon line. My favorite element of the project is the magic that happens when these two parts of the building come together.

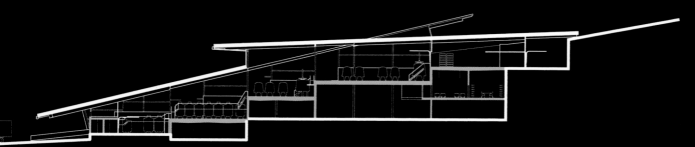

There's a beauty in the function and process of wine making, and Martin's Lane clearly expresses that function.

The Lab

Bellevue, Washington

Situated on a tree-lined boulevard dominated by low-slung 1970s office complexes, this stoic building once housed a lab where a team of laser engineers developed highly classified technologies. The building's industrial envelope appealed to a client seeking offices with gallerylike space in which to curate a substantial art collection, as well as flex space for private events. Converting the building's existing compartmentalized configuration involved equal parts construction and deconstruction. The goal was to retain the building's reserved exterior while lending warmth to its introspective interior by introducing natural light and wood finishes. Stripping the building to its tectonic core and highlighting its original construction, the design reveals and celebrates the patina that has accumulated over time. Ultimately, the architecture is intended to serve as a backdrop to the stunning art displayed within.

disciplined program and
gn solutions that liberate
y-one-acre (eight-hectare)
perched on a bluff with
Valley. The steep slope
e home's cantilevered design,
ound, creating space for
hirty-five-foot-long (eleven-
el ramp begins the dramatic
n a massive, pivoting steel
ght windows in the main living
hat dominate the lot. The
mily to experience the land
he house, connecting with
side.

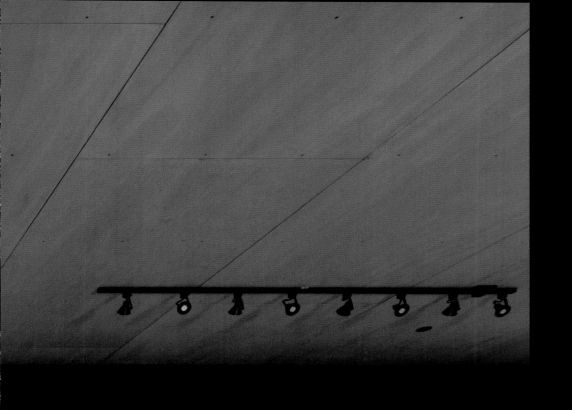

Our strategy with these kinds of houses in remote locations is to make them tough on the outside, soft on the inside, like a Tootsie Pop.

Maxon House had the perfect site for the prospect/refuge balance we're always trying to find in a home location, with the forest behind protecting you and the prospect view out over the valley.

Wagner Education Center,
the Center for Wooden Boats

Seattle, Washington

The Wagner Education Center is part of the Center for Wooden Boats, a Seattle maritime museum founded in 1976. The design for the new Wagner Center was inspired by the wooden boats housed within; it is a functional, straightforward building that serves as an armature for the museum's activities, supporting the display, restoration, and appreciation of wooden boats. The Wagner Center houses a youth classroom that can be converted to a sail loft in the evening for events, new gallery and exhibition space, and a boat shop designed to facilitate the restoration of the museum's largest boats and the construction of new boats from historic designs.

The Wagner Center gives the Center for Wooden Boats a public face, bringing it out of the water and onto the shore and creating transparency between the city of Seattle and the historic boats on nearby Lake Union. A double-height glass window wall and a large covered porch on the restoration hall puts the Center for Wooden Boats' activities on public display, celebrating the historic boats for which it is most beloved. Designed for passive cooling in the relatively mild summer months, the building has no air-conditioning; its occupants interact with it as they would a boat. A movable exterior shade system and operable windows and skylights allow users to tune the building as they might trim the sails of a boat, working with natural forces to optimize performance.

The Center for Wooden Boats has played a critical role in educating the public not just about boats, but also about the value of craft and the forces of nature that surround us. At their core, the boats represent the harnessing of natural forces using only the power of human hands. The new building seeks to reinvigorate this mission and reintroduce the public to the beautifully complex craft of wooden boats.

The architecture of the Wagner Education Center is intended to be a support vehicle for the repair, restoration, and display of boats. It really is a boathouse in the truest sense—it's about the boats, not about the house.

FRED & MIKE
HAYES
CROW'S NEST

Bilgola Beach House

Sydney, Australia

This family home is settled within the sand dunes of Bilgola Beach on the northern coast of Sydney. Responding to the beachfront environment of its headland site, the residence is designed to withstand Australia's dramatic climate conditions: harsh sunlight, high winds, and flooding are common throughout the year. The structure is set on concrete piles, allowing sand and water to move in and out from beneath the building. Shaded retractable window walls provide passive ventilation and merge inside with outside, encouraging the family to connect with the natural environment. An interior courtyard brings filtered daylight into the core of the home, where a central water feature helps to cool the air. The color of the house's board-formed concrete walls references the color of local sand, relating the architecture to its site and helping it merge with the natural condition of the headlands as it weathers over time.

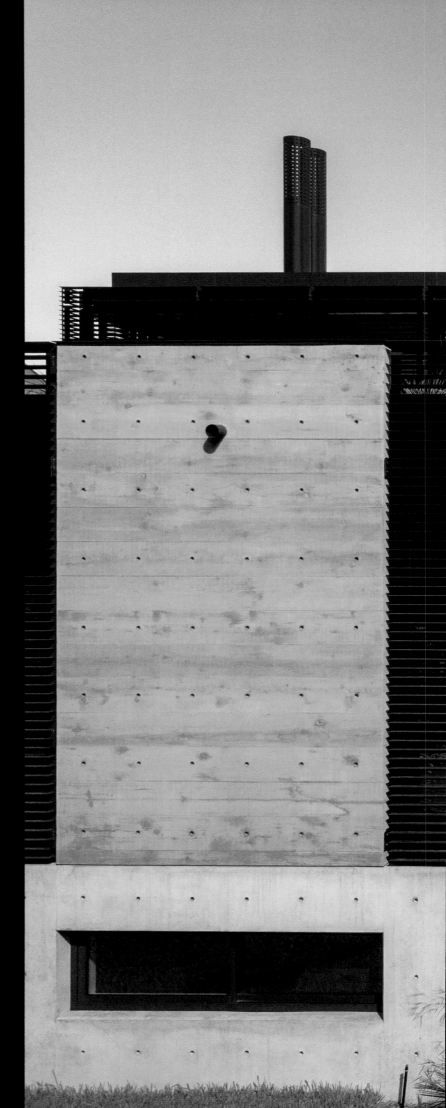

This was my first time working in Australia, and it was an honor and a privilege to be invited to design this special home. The house attempts to address the varied climatic conditions of Australia in the best way, allowing the owners to open or close it to the beachfront as the weather changes.

My hope is that the home will grow and evolve as it responds to all the different environmental and climatic conditions of the site, blending into the headlands and becoming more integrated with Bilgola Beach over time.

Costa Rica Treehouse

Santa Teresa, Costa Rica

Costa Rica Treehouse is inspired by the jungle of its densely forested site. Built entirely of locally harvested teak wood, the retreat engages with the jungle at each of its three levels: the ground floor opens to the forest floor, the middle level is nestled within the trees, and the top level rises above the tree canopy, offering views of the surf at nearby Playa Hermosa.

The clients are surfers as well as avid environmentalists, and this open-air surfer hut reflects their dual interests. The project engages the Costa Rican landscape in various ways, from the vegetation accessible just off the main floor to the larger weather and surf patterns one can experience on the top level. Designed to operate passively, the home can breathe and remain open to the environment. The top and bottom floors open completely to the elements, with a double-screen operable wood-shutter system that admits daylight and natural ventilation but also provides privacy and security when the owners are away. Shading, a 3.5-kilowatt photovoltaic array, and a rainwater collection system make the house's compact footprint even lighter on the land.

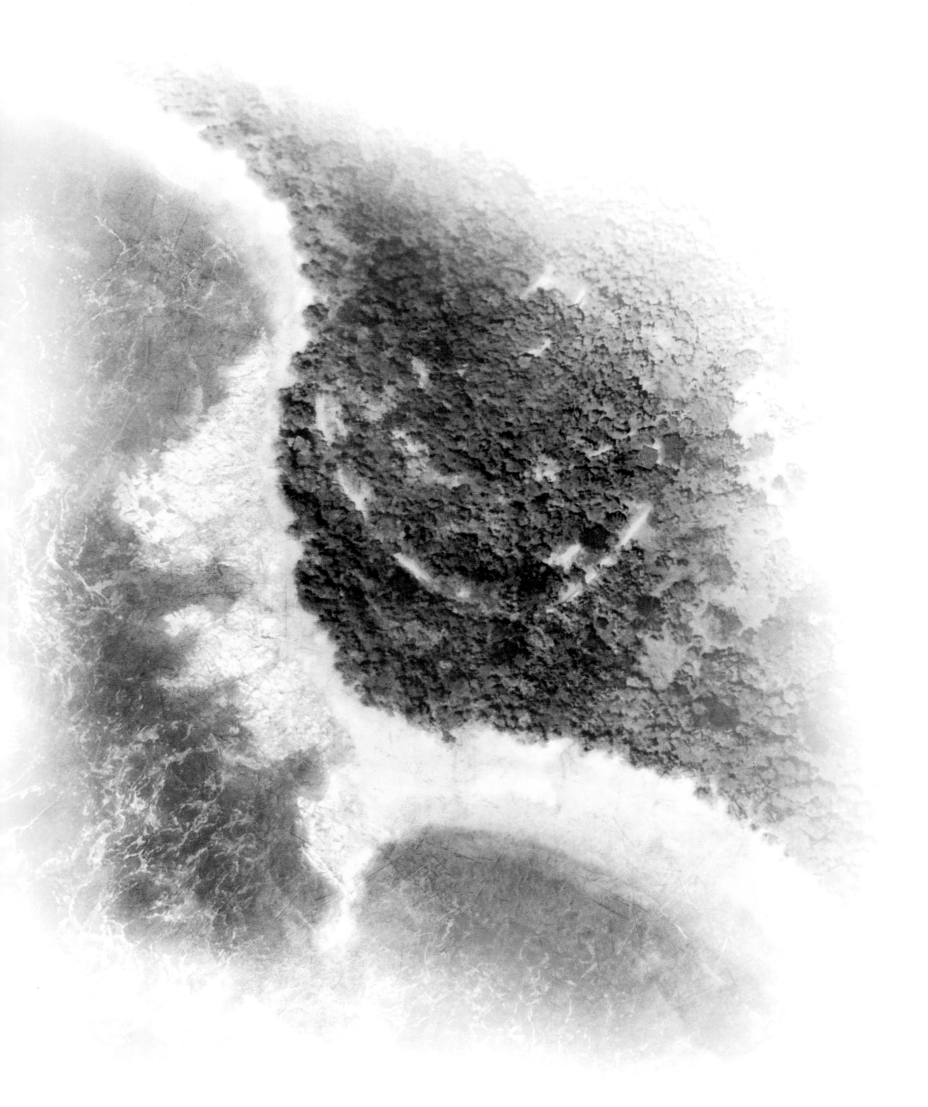

The house is intended
to breathe and open
to the climate as
much as possible.

The project has a relatively light, natural footprint on the landscape, not only in terms of the site itself, but also in using available local materials that are helping advance the next level of environmental stewardship in Costa Rica.

9th & Thomas

Seattle, Washington

This site was originally developed in 1944 as the headquarters of Sellen Construction, a locally owned general contractor in the Pacific Northwest. The Redman family, owners of Sellen, decided to develop this legacy project after their headquarters moved around the corner in 1999. Their agenda was twofold: to create a family project emblematic of their history and to invest in their neighborhood by creating a central community hub. The building's lobby, or "living room," contains retail and gathering spaces designed to make people feel like they're at home.

The building's design emphasizes porosity and adaptability. The podium level is articulated in an eclectic style that references the evolutionary process of a community; the parts and pieces of its transparent volume move and change, open and close. The design is also sensitive to the pedestrian scale of the neighborhood: setbacks, exposed terraces, and inset, covered terraces on nearly every floor help break down the building's scale, making it responsive to its context at all levels. Operable windows allow the building to dress for Seattle's ever-changing weather conditions and enhance the indoor/outdoor relationship that is so important in the region's mild climate.

Wasatch House

Salt Lake City, Utah

The main idea behind this residence was to split it into three pavilions that separate the various functions of the home. A public, formal area at the front of the house can accommodate large gatherings; a transitional middle zone contains gathering space for the family; and a more private, intimate realm provides a retreat at the opposite end of the house, where the bedrooms are.

   The design creates a close relationship between the architecture and the natural environment, with the landscape weaving around and under the home. Views of the Oquirrh Mountains to the west and Wasatch Range to the east informed its orientation, particularly the master bedroom, whose roof bears a small kick that provides an unobstructed view of Mount Olympus.

The smaller and more pavilion-like
the buildings are, the more the natural
landscape feels close by.

I wanted to create a home that would not only respond to the way the family lives now, but also be able to grow and change over time. The home's layout allows the family to modify the building in response to an unforeseen future.

The Bo Bartlett Center

Columbus, Georgia

A former cotton warehouse on the banks of the Chattahoochee River, the Bo Bartlett Center is a multidisciplinary gallery, archive, and educational space at Columbus State University. The goal of the design was to create a space where the architecture disappears and the work of the Columbus-born painter Bo Bartlett lights up the place.

The space needed to volumetrically meet the scale of Bartlett's work, which varies from small sketches and memorabilia to eight-foot-wide (two-meter-wide) paintings. The center houses more than three hundred paintings and drawings by Bartlett as well as his complete archive of sketchbooks, correspondence, journals, photographs, and art objects. The design reveals the original warehouse structure and leaves it raw, with unfinished concrete floors and exposed steel beams in the twenty-three-foot-high (seven-meter-high) ceilings. Kinetic gallery walls allow the plan and circulation to be adapted and rearranged so that the center can accommodate many types of exhibitions and programs. Ultimately, the architecture takes a supporting role, highlighting Bartlett's work so visitors can focus on his paintings and his legacy.

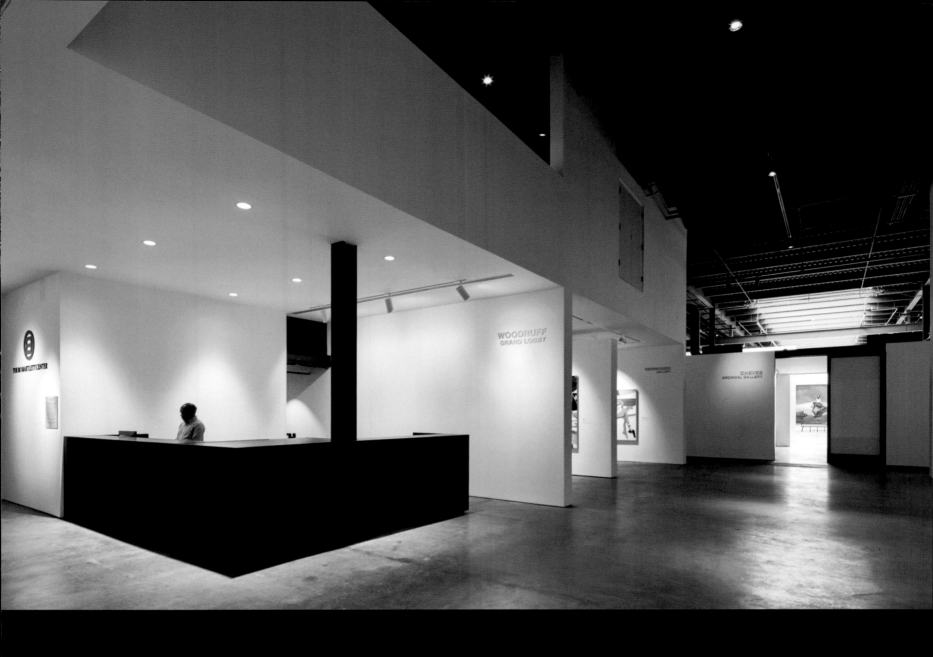

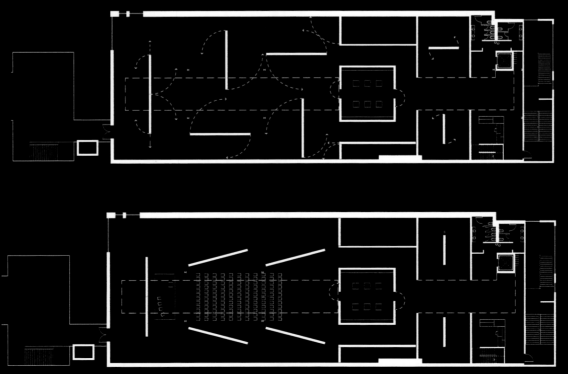

Bo is a friend first and foremost, and he's an artistic force of nature. I have a deep respect for his work. My goal as architect was to frame Bo's work as best as possible so visitors can focus on what he is putting into his paintings.

Collywood

West Hollywood, California

Sited on a hill overlooking the Sunset Strip, this high-tech West Hollywood home overlooks Los Angeles, with views stretching from the San Gabriel Mountains to the Pacific Ocean. This big view—with all its varying personalities, depending on time of day and weather—was the key design driver. The client comes from a background of outdoor adventures. He wanted the house to feel like an adventure as he and his many guests walk through its 15,600 square feet (1,450 square meters) on three levels.

The boundary between inside and outside is all but dissolved, with living spaces that open completely to nearly 7,000 square feet (650 square meters) of terraces, gardens, and pools. The dining area opens on both sides via a pair of guillotine window walls, and there are several more retractable window walls throughout the living area, kitchen, and bedrooms. Like a Rubik's Cube of interlocking boxes and planes, the home balances multiple scales, from intimate handcrafted interior moments to the sweeping, dynamic LA cityscape.

Because the home is located in California, there's a strong indoor/outdoor connection. Terraces become outdoor living areas, and indoor rooms open up completely, almost erasing the line between inside and outside.

Burke Museum of Natural History and Culture

Seattle, Washington

The oldest public museum in Washington State, the Burke Museum of Natural History and Culture has a collection of more than sixteen million artifacts and specimens, ranging from totem poles and gemstones to dinosaur fossils. Because the Burke's holdings are so wide-ranging and continue to grow (it is a collecting museum), the new building needed to serve as a coherent, effective, and flexible container. The building's rational scheme accommodates the complexity of the Burke's activities and collections, both current and future.

A key design goal was to create maximum transparency, exposing every part of the Burke and incorporating it into the visitor experience. The design breaks down traditional museum barriers between public and "back-of-house" spaces, integrating collections and research labs with traditional galleries. Dual entrances link the museum to its context, connecting to both the University of Washington campus and the surrounding community. A twenty-four-by-twenty-foot (seven-by-six-meter) pivoting window wall continues the emphasis on transparency to literally open the Burke to the nature of a new outdoor courtyard. At its core, the mission of the Burke is to help everyone—curators, educators, students, and the general public—make a connection with our natural world in all its complexities.

We wanted to create a simple, beautiful, rational, and flexible building that will serve the Burke for hundreds of years. It is an inviting place—not only for the public but also for the scientists, researchers, and curators of today and tomorrow.

The design goal was to tell the story of the Burke through transparency, allowing the public to see inside to every part of the museum, revealing elements like research and collections management that were previously hidden from view.

CheckMate Winery Pop-Up

Oliver, British Columbia

At 575 square feet (53 square meters), this transformable structure was originally conceived as a prototype for a collection of rentable vacation cabins or seasonal worker housing. For now, the prototype will function as a pop-up tasting room, serving CheckMate Winery's long-standing goal of bringing awareness to the high-quality wines produced in the region.

Essentially a steel-and-glass box, the prototype is enclosed by perforated, corrugated metal shutters on three sides that will patina over time. These shutters can be manually raised via a system of gas springs and double as shading roofs for the exterior deck when open. Sized to fit on a standard flatbed truck, the structure incorporates lifting lugs so it can be easily moved to any number of future locations.

The idea is that the building should feel like it fits wherever it goes—in the Okanagan Valley or beyond—because it's able to morph in shape and use.

at adjacent to Tijuca National Park outside of
 rational steel-and-glass box supported by
s. The 1,200-square-foot (111-square-meter)
he rain forest canopy—a secluded hideaway
couple can retreat from the city and connect
andscape.

 sited in harmony with the wildness of its
ting. Tucked into the trees, the north end of
s a single bedroom, while the south end opens
ea, and Rio's famous Christ the Redeemer
creened porch and outdoor kitchenette allow
gage with the landscape.

ine-grade stainless structural steel—the home's
—stands up to the humid climate, where corro-
 Manual gizmos on pivot windows and retract-
s, as well as a solar water-heating system, allow
ion during intermittent power outages. Local
niques are incorporated inside and outside the
-formed concrete site walls and colorful plaster
he Brazilian wood and *vermelhão*-stained
common vernacular tradition.

This house is a private, intimate place for the owner couple to go up into the hillside above Rio de Janeiro and enjoy books, art, and especially the landscape.

The agenda was simple: to make the house as small as possible in the big, beautiful landscape of the Tijuca jungle.

Teton House

Jackson Hole, Wyoming

A true mountain home, Teton House embraces the dramatically varied climate in Jackson Hole. The clients wanted to engage the achingly beautiful landscape but also be able to shutter the home when away or during challenging bouts of weather.

The home acts as a launching platform for the family to engage with nature during all four seasons, with a ski-in/ski-out element, a bike shop, and a detached guest hut for smaller groups to use without needing to open up the main home. With its large window walls, the house stretches the traditional boundaries of transparency for a mountain home, but it can also be extremely protective when its exterior wood shutter system is closed via several hand-cranked pulleys. Warm wood interiors of rift-cut oak, fir, and walnut create softly nuanced interior moments—the duality of the big, dramatic landscape just outside.

Comedor Restaurant

Austin, Texas

The design for Comedor, a modern Mexican restaurant in downtown Austin, creates a sanctuary on a busy urban intersection. The new building takes a strong corner position to leave space for a protected open-air inner courtyard. Incorporating glass brick on the street-facing portions communicates in a mysterious way what is happening inside the restaurant, bar, and courtyard to the passing traffic and pedestrians.

Quiet from the outside, this urban oasis transports visitors once inside. The heart of Comedor is the courtyard, with its paloverde and acacia trees and a small fountain. Discovered during construction, the over-one-hundred-year-old exposed brick from the adjacent historical McGarrah Jessee Building lends texture and context to the courtyard, which opens to the elements to take advantage of Austin's climate. The interior double-height, glass-wrapped dining space adjoins the courtyard via four retractable guillotine window walls operated by hand cranks, allowing Comedor to open completely to the courtyard.

Chemin Byron

Geneva, Switzerland

This house is in a traditional Swiss neighborhood on the out-skirts of Geneva. Carefully integrated into its steeply sloped site, the home balances a modern architectural language with a warm, intimate feel. Because the team worked closely with local builders and engineers, the house incorporates the high level of craftsmanship and precision for which Swiss architecture is known. This collaboration is also reflected in the exterior materials: steel and glass are finished with traditional locally sourced terra-cotta and European pine. Taking advantage of its hillside site, the three-story home opens to views of Lake Geneva and the Jura Mountains. The covered terrace contains a figural sculpture by Antony Gormley that draws the eye outdoors toward the gardens, lap pool, and lake beyond.

This was my first project in Switzerland, which was exciting because I'm a Swiss citizen. I spent a few years in Switzerland during my childhood and have important family connections there. It's my homeland, in a sense, and I was excited to be returning home for this project.

Tillamook Creamery Visitor Center

Tillamook, Oregon

The new Tillamook Creamery Visitor Center is the latest addition to Tillamook's Oregon coast campus, which has seen many phases of development since the original factory building opened in 1947. The goal of the expansion and addition was to reference Tillamook's agricultural tradition with a rational, straightforward building that felt true to the experience and history of the farmers who make up the Tillamook cooperative.

Adjacent to Tillamook's flagship manufacturing facility, the Visitor Center contains interpretive exhibits, a retail shop, a restaurant, an ice cream counter, and an adjacent lawn. Drawing on local agricultural vernacular, the building is a modern barn structure with a simple shed roof. The landscape contains grasses, shrubs, and trees native to the Oregon coast. Inside, exhibits allow Tillamook Creamery to share its traditions, processes, and products with more than 1.3 million visitors every year.

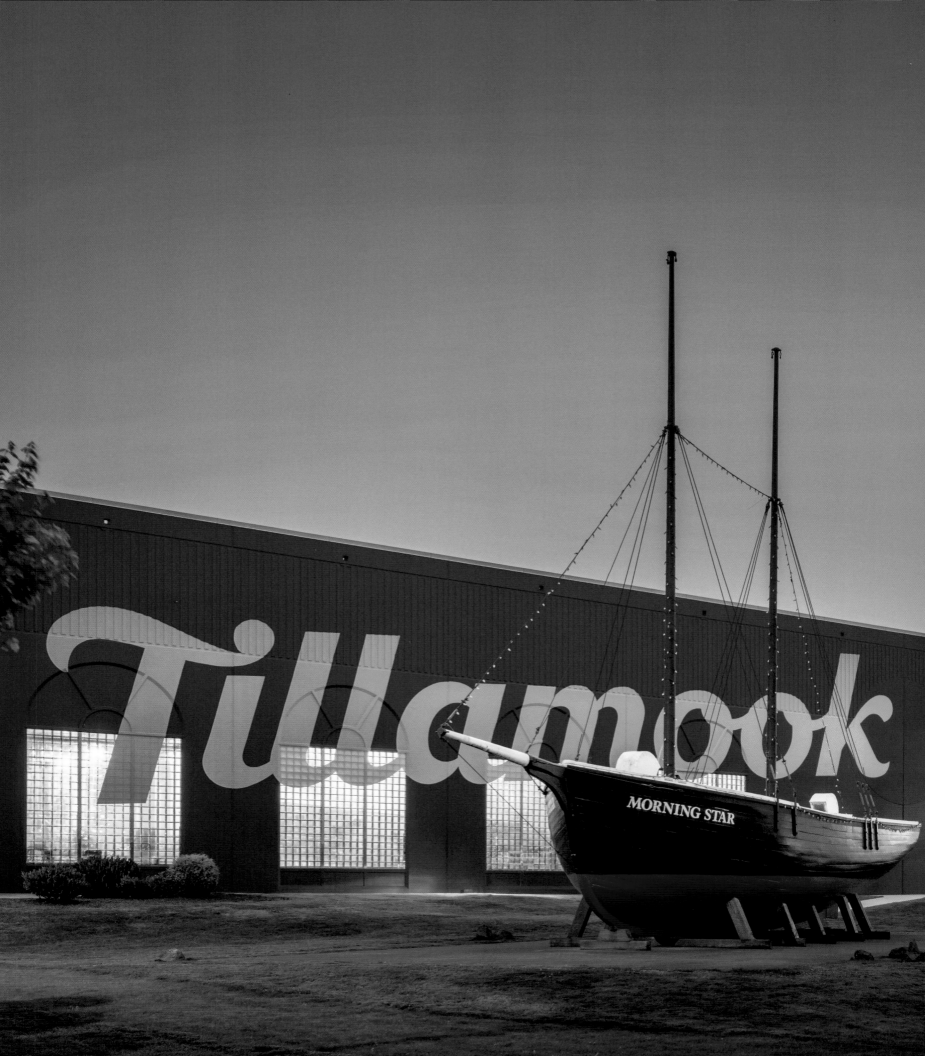

Our hope is that the new building and
the experiences visitors have within will
become part of the Tillamook story—a

Dragonfly

Whitefish, Montana

Situated on the ecotone between a ponderosa pine forest and Whitefish Lake in northwestern Montana, this vacation home is a framework for the owners to experience nature. The house emphasizes the crossing point between these two ecological zones—a distinct yet subtle marker of the family's presence and legacy.

     The site has been a longtime vacation spot for the family, who camped there before their home was built; the house was designed to maintain the sense of natural discovery the family had enjoyed when spending time on the land. Multiple outdoor living spaces offer varying levels of enclosure, allowing the family to engage with nature during all seasons. The site plan is organized around a path leading through the forest and down to the lake. Along the way, covered decks, a firepit, and a hot pool nestled into the hillside chart a path of discovery from house to lake.

The house can dress to the climate—it's designed to be used during all four seasons. It transitions from a protected refuge to a semienclosed condition to an exposed prospect situation open to the lake.

Like a dragonfly, this house sits lightly on the land and disappears into the landscape. It quietly emerges out of the forest and overlooks the lake below.

Millerton Farmhouse

Millerton, New York

Located on twenty-five acres (ten hectares) of farmland in upstate New York, this family retreat is a modern take on the traditional farmhouse. The home is a touchstone for the couple who own it and their extended family; it is designed as a series of buildings attached by covered walkways and interstitial spaces to accommodate large family gatherings but still retain an intimate feel. Attention to spatial and volumetric relationships makes the home both modern and contextually appropriate for its Hudson Valley farmland setting. It combines contemporary detailing and materials like blackened steel and concrete with vernacular agricultural building forms and materials. The siding is reclaimed wood sourced from local historic barns that had been dismantled, and the roofs are corrugated zinc.

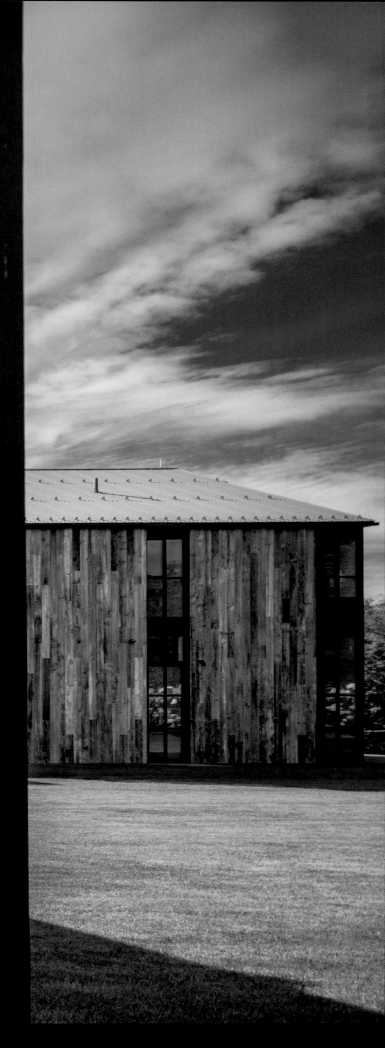

The house had to feel like it fit into the farmland vernacular of upstate New York, but with a modern architectural language.

The house flows very naturally into the landscape and into the dynamics of this growing, evolving family.

100 Stewart Hotel & Apartments

Seattle, Washington

Located adjacent to the Pike Place Market Historical District, 100 Stewart Hotel & Apartments is neighbored by buildings that represent Seattle's rich history. For that reason, a central design consideration was the scale of the new structure and its relationship to the smaller, older buildings in the area as well as the historic development grid of the property. The site's position at a major axial grid shift, where First Avenue bends to align with the city's topography, presented a unique opportunity to mark this significant intersection and create a gateway between neighborhoods.

The building is composed of two primary elements that break up the expression of the structure: a focal-point "glass lantern" with geometric offsets that physically mimic the street grid, and an adjoining frame of solid facades that provides a visual counterpoint and folds the building into its context. The development reflects the pedestrian-oriented character of the Pike Place Market Historical District with an interior courtyard that connects to existing pedestrian pathways, offering a sheltered space of respite. The eleven-story hotel both commands and honors the site, transforming from a semitransparent crystal box by day into an illuminated sanctuary by night.

In response to the special corner lot where the grid shifts, we explored the connection between large, public views and more intimate, personal views.

Acknowledgments

Many talented individuals contributed to the projects contained in this book. I am grateful to my clients for taking a leap of faith with me and encouraging opportunities for experimentation. I also want to thank the contractors, craftspeople, and artists who helped bring these projects to life. To my project teams: thank you for working tirelessly together toward our collective success.

This book would not have been possible without the help of many people: MacKenzie Cotters, Gabriela Frank, Ciara Cronin, Lauren Gallow, Evan Harlan, Jonnie Nelson, Miko McGinty, Rebecca Sylvers, and everyone at Princeton Architectural Press. Thank you to Mark Rozzo and Michael Chaiken for your insights and illuminating conversations. It has been an honor working together with all of you toward a single, common goal.

Chronology of Projects

Vinegar Flats Development
Spokane, Washington

Westlake Hills Residence
Austin, Texas

Whitefish Lakehouse
Whitefish, Montana

Wilson
Jackson, Wyoming

XSENSOR Technology
Headquarters
Calgary, Alberta

Yellowstone Club
Big Sky, Montana

2019

9th & Thomas
Seattle, Washington

9th & Thomas Residence
Seattle, Washington

Art Los Angeles Contemporary
Santa Monica, California

Burke Museum of Natural History
and Culture
Seattle, Washington

Comedor Restaurant
Austin, Texas

Farmer's Park Greenhouse
Anaheim, California

Hornall Anderson Offices
Seattle, Washington

Portola Valley Residence
Portola Valley, California

Puerto Cancun Residence
Puerto Cancun, Mexico

Wagner Education Center,
the Center for Wooden Boats
Seattle, Washington

2018

Bilgola Beach House
Sydney, Australia

Collywood
West Hollywood, California

Hale Lana
Kona, Hawaii

JW Marriott Seoul Renewal
Seoul, South Korea

Leschi Inventor
Seattle, Washington

Montauk Residence
Montauk, New York

MrSteam
Long Island City, New York

Olson Kundig Office Renovation
Seattle, Washington

Rio House
Rio de Janeiro, Brazil

St. Mark's Cathedral Expansion
and Renovation
Seattle, Washington

Tacoma Art Museum
Benaroya Wing
Tacoma, Washington

Teton House
Jackson Hole, Wyoming

Tillamook Creamery Visitor Center
Tillamook, Oregon

Vermont Cabin
Stowe, Vermont

West Edge Tower
Seattle, Washington

2017

The Bo Bartlett Center
Columbus, Georgia

CheckMate Winery Pop-Up
Oliver, British Columbia

Chemin Byron
Geneva, Switzerland

Chilmark House
Martha's Vineyard, Massachusetts

Costa Rica Treehouse
Santa Teresa, Costa Rica

North Fork Residence Remodel
Long Island, New York

River House
Ketchum, Idaho

Saratoga Residence
Saratoga, California

Triptych
Yarrow Point, Washington

2016

100 Stewart Hotel & Apartments
Seattle, Washington

Dallas Apartment
Dallas, Texas

Deer Run
Ketchum, Idaho

Dragonfly
Whitefish, Montana

Martin's Lane Winery
Kelowna, British Columbia

Maxon House
Carnation, Washington

Meg Home
Seattle, Washington

Millerton Farmhouse
Millerton, New York

San Juan Island Home
Friday Harbor, Washington

Wasatch House
Salt Lake City, Utah

2015

Berkeley Residence
Berkeley, California

Charles Smith Wines Jet City
Seattle, Washington

Heritage University Master Plan
Toppenish, Washington

Hollywood Hills Residence
Los Angeles, California

The Lab
Bellevue, Washington

Leschi House
Seattle, Washington

Optimism Brewery
Seattle, Washington

Outpost Basel at Design
Miami/ Basel
Basel, Switzerland

Paradise Road Housing,
Smith College
Northampton, Massachusetts

Park City Cabin (unbuilt)
Park City, Utah

Point Reyes Retreat (unbuilt)
Point Reyes, California

Shinsegae International
Seoul, South Korea

Stirrup House
Ketchum, Idaho

2014

242 State Street
Los Altos, California

Berkshire Residence
New Marlborough, Massachusetts

Heritage University, Art Building,
Student Services Building, and
Classroom Building
Toppenish, Washington

Hulen Meadows Residence
Ketchum, Idaho

Naramata Barn and Garage
Naramata, British Columbia

NYC Residence
New York, New York

Pieso Poagen
Nine Mile Falls, Washington

Presidio Gateway
(competition entry)
San Francisco, California

Recreation Barn
Santa Barbara, California

Rimrock
Spokane, Washington

Sawmill
Tehachapi, California

Spokane Riverfront Master Plan
Spokane, Washington

Tacoma Art Museum,
Haub Gallery Addition
Tacoma, Washington

Upper East Side Residence
New York, New York

West Seattle Bluff Residence
Seattle, Washington

Whistler Ski House
Whistler, British Columbia

Wolfeboro Residence
Wolfeboro, New Hampshire

2013

Benton City Farm
Benton City, Washington

Kapa'a Residence
Kauai, Hawaii

Kuruma House Remodel
Seattle, Washington

Live Oak Residence
Los Angeles, California

Pole Pass Cabin
Orcas Island, Washington

Santa Barbara Residence
Santa Barbara, California

Substance Winery
Seattle, Washington

Sun Valley Center for the Arts
(unbuilt)
Ketchum, Idaho

2012

BAK House
Buenos Aires, Argentina

Cascade Apartment/Gallery
Seattle, Washington

Dynamite Shed
Ketchum, Idaho

Hawaii Residence
Kona, Hawaii

Mt. Bonnell Residence (unbuilt)
Austin, Texas

Studhorse
Winthrop, Washington

2011

Bridlewood Winery Master Plan
(unbuilt)
Santa Ynez, California

Canal Residence (unbuilt)
Venice, California

Charles Smith Wines Tasting Room
and World Headquarters
Walla Walla, Washington

Epoch Estate Wines (unbuilt)
Templeton, California

Le Massif de Charlevoix (unbuilt)
Baie St. Paul, Quebec

Sol Duc Cabin
Olympic Peninsula, Washington

Tansu House
Seattle, Washington

2010

Art Stable
Seattle, Washington

Border Crossing, Fallingwater
(competition entry)
Bear Run, Pennsylvania

East Village Apartment
New York, New York

False Bay Writer's Cabin
San Juan Island, Washington

Lake Okanagan Residence
Lake Country, British Columbia

Laurelhurst Residence
Seattle, Washington

Madison Park Residence
Seattle, Washington

Mission Hill Family Estate Winery
Westbank, British Columbia

Mountain Residence (unbuilt)
Roslyn, Washington

Outpost Ranch Cabin
Pincher Creek, Alberta

The Pierre
Lopez Island, Washington

Private Estate
Seattle, Washington

SOMA Tower (competition entry)
Bellevue, Washington

Stadium Nissan of Seattle
Seattle, Washington

Studio Sitges
Sitges, Spain

West Chelsea Apartment
New York, New York

2009

1111 E. Pike
Seattle, Washington

Belmont Residence
Vancouver, British Columbia

Bryce Canyon Resort (unbuilt)
Bryce Canyon, Utah

Chat-O Spapho
Lopez Island, Washington

Contemplating the Void,
Guggenheim Museum
(exhibition entry)
New York, New York

Fashion Climber, *W* Magazine
(competition entry)
New York, New York

Georgetown Brewing Company
Seattle, Washington

Hammer House
Seattle, Washington

Lucky Bench Residence
Ancramdale, New York

Mike's Hard Lemonade
Headquarters
Seattle, Washington

Mistral Restaurant
Seattle, Washington

Puget Sound Residence
Seattle, Washington

Riley's Cove Residence Remodel
Mercer Island, Washington

Shadowboxx
Lopez Island, Washington

Slaughterhouse Beach House
Maui, Hawaii

T Bailey Office Building (unbuilt)
Anacortes, Washington

2008

Altis Resort
Mammoth Lakes, California

Breckenridge Cabin (unbuilt)
Breckenridge, Colorado

Gulf Islands Cabin
Gulf Islands, British Columbia

Highlands House
Highlands, North Carolina

Madison Street Condominiums
(unbuilt)
Seattle, Washington

Outpost
Bellevue, Idaho

Scramble Tower (unbuilt)
New York, New York

Tofino Lodge (unbuilt)
Vancouver Island, British Columbia

2007

Atherton House
Atherton, California

Mercer Island Residence
Mercer Island, Washington

Milepost 45.6 (unbuilt)
Valdez, Alaska

Montecito Residence
Montecito, California

Mount Royal Residence
Calgary, Alberta

Portland Hilltop House
Portland, Oregon

Rolling Huts
Mazama, Washington

SoBECA Development
Project C, Costa Mesa, California

West Rim House
Spokane, Washington

2006

Artist's Studio
Seattle, Washington

Femme Osage Farm (unbuilt)
St. Charles County, Missouri

Fremont Houseboat (unbuilt)
Seattle, Washington

Hot Rod House
Seattle, Washington

Island Pool House
San Juan Islands, Washington

Lightning Ridge Residence (unbuilt)
Portland, Oregon

West Edge Condominium
Seattle, Washington

2005

Capitol Hill Residence
Seattle, Washington

Inn at Cave B
George, Washington

Island Shop Remodel
Bainbridge, Washington

Pratt Fine Arts Center Study (unbuilt)
Seattle, Washington

Publicis Seattle Office
Seattle, Washington

Queen Anne Residence
Seattle, Washington

Sagecliffe Resort (unbuilt)
George, Washington

Tye River Cabin
Skykomish, Washington

2004

Cambridge Mesh (competition entry)
Boston, Massachusetts

Davenport District Master Plan
Spokane, Washington

Mercer Island Ridge Residence
Mercer Island, Washington

Mission Hill Family Estate Winery (exhibition entry)
Westbank, British Columbia

Mount Si Residence
North Bend, Washington

Olson Kundig Architects Offices
Seattle, Washington

Ranch House
Miles City, Montana

Shamrock Residence Remodel
Vancouver, British Columbia

Summit Law Group Office
Seattle, Washington

Winston Wachter Gallery
Seattle, Washington

2003

Beach House (unbuilt)
Sarasota, Florida

Bulldozer Camp (unbuilt)
Dusty, Washington

Chicken Point Cabin
Hayden Lake, Idaho

Meydenbauer Bay Residence
Bellevue, Washington

Seattle Art Museum, Rental Gallery
Seattle, Washington

Ski Condo
Vail, Colorado

S/W Condominium Remodel
Seattle, Washington

Vashon Studio (unbuilt)
Vashon Island, Washington

2002

Belmont Coach House
Vancouver, British Columbia

Delta Shelter
Mazama, Washington

Lake Residence Remodel
Seattle, Washington

Madrona Residence
Seattle, Washington

Meadow Studio
Vashon Island, Washington

Private Estate
Mercer Island, Washington

Sedgwick Road Office
Seattle, Washington

Steel Residence (unbuilt)
Anacortes, Washington

Tsunami Residence
Medina, Washington

2001

Courtyard House
Juanita, Washington

Dishman Hills Residence
Spokane, Washington

Liberty Heights Residence (unbuilt)
San Francisco, California

Mica Bay Residence
Coeur d'Alene, Idaho

Millennium Tower Condominium (unit design)
Seattle, Washington

Mission Hill Family Estate Winery, 02 Warehouse
Westbank, British Columbia

Mission Hill Family Estate Winery, Vineyard Cottages
Westbank, British Columbia

North Seattle Residence Remodel
Seattle, Washington

Ridge House
Spokane, Washington

2000

55 Bell Street Offices and Condominiums (unbuilt)
Seattle, Washington

The Catholic Newman Center, University of Washington
Seattle, Washington

Hill House Residence
Mercer Island, Washington

Mission Hill Family Estate Winery
Westbank, British Columbia

Osoyoos Barn and Visitor Center
Oliver, British Columbia

Tree House Residence (unbuilt)
Portola Valley, California

West Mercer Residence (unbuilt)
Mercer Island, Washington

Woodside Ranch (unbuilt)
Woodside, California

1999

Alaska Aviation Heritage Museum (conceptual design)
Anchorage, Alaska

Chapel of St. Ignatius, Seattle University (associate to Steven Holl Architects)
Seattle, Washington

Lake Travis Residence (unbuilt)
Austin, Texas

Portage Bay Residence 2
Seattle, Washington

1998

Courtyard House
Bellevue, Washington

Dash Point Residence
Federal Way, Washington

Gray Point Cabin
Coeur d'Alene, Idaho

Haro Strait Residence
San Juan Island, Washington

Highland Condominium
Seattle, Washington

Highland Condominium 2
Seattle, Washington

Leschi Residence
Seattle, Washington

Orchard Residence (unbuilt)
Chelan, Washington

Overturf Residence Remodel
Bellevue, Washington

Rainshadow Residence (unbuilt)
Sequim, Washington

Studio House
Seattle, Washington

Valdez Maritime Cultural Center (concept study)
Valdez, Alaska

1997

Blue Ridge Residence Remodel
Seattle, Washington

Ketchum Inn Hotel, Master Plan (unbuilt)
Ketchum, Idaho

Shelter House (with Jim Olson)
Mercer Island, Washington

1996

Charter Construction Office Remodel
Seattle, Washington

Palouse Residence (unbuilt)
Spokane, Washington

1995

Beach Residence (unbuilt)
Mercer Island, Washington

Cougar Mountain Residence (unbuilt)
Bellevue, Washington

Lakeridge Heights
Bellevue, Washington

1994

Forest Residence
Marrowstone Island, Washington

Hunt's Point Residence Remodel
Hunt's Point, Washington

Issaquah Eco Center (unbuilt)
Issaquah, Washington

1993

Cannon Beach Cabin (unbuilt)
Cannon Beach, Oregon

Madison Park Condominium
Seattle, Washington

1992

Bluff House (with Jim Olson)
Seattle, Washington

City House (with Jim Olson)
Seattle, Washington

Meadow Residence
Kirkland, Washington

Ranch House
Ellensburg, Washington

1990

Home House (unbuilt)
Home, Washington

Monroe Jewelers
Seattle, Washington

Publication Services Building, University of Washington
Seattle, Washington

Steven's Court Housing, University of Washington (competition entry)
Seattle, Washington

1989

Federal Way Residence
Federal Way, Washington

Tacoma Actors Guild
Tacoma, Washington

Waterfront Residence (with Jim Olson)
Seattle, Washington

1987

Burberry's of London
Seattle, Washington

Professional Notes

Selected Awards

2019

Architectural Digest, AD100, Olson Kundig
Fast Company, Top 10 Most Innovative Companies in Architecture, Olson Kundig
University of Washington Department of Architecture Distinguished Alumni Award, Tom Kundig

2018

AIA National Committee on the Environment, Top Ten Award, Sawmill
AIA National Honor Award, Small Projects, Honor Award, Sawmill
AIA Seattle Medal of Honor, Tom Kundig
Architectural Digest, AD100, Olson Kundig
Chicago Athenaeum, American Architecture Award, 100 Stewart Hotel & Apartments
Chicago Athenaeum, American Architecture Award, Dragonfly

2017

AIA National Housing Award, Sawmill
AIA Northwest and Pacific Region Design Award, Citation Award, Martin's Lane Winery
AIA Northwest and Pacific Region Design Award, Citation Award, Sawmill
AIA Seattle Honor Award, Merit Award, 100 Stewart Hotel & Apartments
Architectural Digest, AD100, Olson Kundig
Architectural Record, Record House, Meg Home
Architectural Record, Top 300 Firms, Olson Kundig
Chicago Athenaeum, American Architecture Award, Charles Smith Wines Jet City
Chicago Athenaeum, American Architecture Award, Martin's Lane Winery
Chicago Athenaeum, American Architecture Award, Sawmill
Chicago Athenaeum, American Architecture Award, Honor Award, Shinsegae International
Historic Seattle Preservation Award, Neighborhood Reinvestment, Optimism Brewing
Royal Institute of British Architects Fellowship, Tom Kundig
World Architecture News, Tall Buildings Award, Shinsegae International

2016

AIA Northwest and Pacific Region Honor Award, Shinsegae International

AIA Seattle Honor Award, Martin's Lane Winery
Architectural Digest, AD100, Olson Kundig
Architectural Record, Top 300 Firms, Olson Kundig
Architizer A+Award, Building Products: Hardware, Tom Kundig Collection
Architizer A+ Award, Commercial: Office—Mid Rise (5–15 Floors), Jury Winner, Shinsegae International
Architizer A+Award, Hospitality: Bars & Nightclubs, Charles Smith Wines Jet City
Architizer A+Award, Popular Choice, Details: Architecture + Facades, 242 State Street
Chicago Athenaeum, American Architectural Award, Pole Pass Retreat
Council on Tall Buildings and Urban Habitat: Best Tall Building Award, Best Tall Building Asia & Australia, finalist, Shinsegae International
National Academician inductee, Tom Kundig
Ocean Home, Top 50 Coastal Architects of 2016, Olson Kundig

2015

AIA National Housing Award, Studhorse
AIA Seattle Honor Award, Shinsegae International
AIA Washington Civic Design Award, Merit Award, Tacoma Art Museum Haub Galleries
Architectural Digest, AD100, Olson Kundig
Architizer A+Award, finalist, Tom Kundig Collection

2014

AIA National Honor Award, Architecture, The Pierre
AIA National Honor Award, Interior Architecture, The Pierre
AIA National Housing Award, Sol Duc Cabin
Architectural Digest, AD100, Olson Kundig

2013

AIA National Honor Award, Architecture, Art Stable
AIA National Honor Award, Interior Architecture, Charles Smith Wines Tasting Room and World Headquarters
Architizer A+Award, Popular Choice, finalist, Residential Mid Rise (5–15 Floors), Art Stable
Architizer A+Award, Popular Choice, finalist, Residential Single-Family Home, The Pierre
Architizer A+Award, Popular Choice, Special Mention for Retail, Charles Smith Wines Tasting Room and World Headquarters

Chicago Athenaeum, American Architecture Award, Charles Smith Wines Tasting Room and World Headquarters
Residential Architect Design Award, Grand Award for Custom Home / More Than 3,000 Square Feet, Studio Sitges
World Interiors News Award, Interior Accessories, finalist, Tom Kundig Collection

2012

AIA National Housing Award, The Pierre
AIA Northwest and Pacific Region Honor Award, The Pierre
AIA Seattle Honor Award, Citation Award, Shadowboxx Bathhouse
AIA Seattle Honor Award, Commendation Award, Charles Smith Wines Tasting Room and World Headquarters
AIA Seattle Honor Award, Commendation Award, Tansu House
AIA Seattle Honor Award, The Pierre
Builder's Choice Design & Planning Award, Builder's Choice Grand Award, The Pierre
Builder's Choice Design & Planning Award, Builder's Choice Special Focus, Shadowboxx Bathhouse
Chicago Athenaeum, American Architecture Award, Studio Sitges
Chicago Athenaeum, American Architecture Award, The Pierre
European Centre and Chicago Athenaeum International Architecture Award, Art Stable
National Society for Marketing Professional Services Awards, 3rd Place: Book/Monograph, *Tom Kundig: Houses 2*
IIDA Northern Pacific Chapter INaward, People's Choice Award, Charles Smith Wines Tasting Room and World Headquarters
Interior Design magazine Best of Year Award, Tom Kundig Collection
Interior Design magazine Hall of Fame, inducted, Tom Kundig
IIDA Interior Design Award, Best of Competition, The Pierre
Residential Architect Design Award, Architectural Detail Merit Award, Shadowboxx
Residential Architect Design Award, Architectural Detail Merit Award, Studio Sitges
Washington Main Street Program Award, Outstanding Design or Rehabilitation Project Award, Charles Smith Wines Tasting Room and World Headquarters

2011

AIA National Housing Award, 1111 E. Pike
AIA National Housing Award, Art Stable
AIA Northwest and Pacific Region Honor Award, Art Stable
AIA Seattle Merit Award, Sol Duc Cabin
AIA Seattle Honor Award, Art Stable
AIA Seattle and *Northwest Home* magazine Home of the Month, Riley's Cove Residence
Northwest Design Awards, Exotic Retreats category, The Pierre
Residential Architect Design Award, Grand Award, Slaughterhouse Beach House
Residential Architect Design Award, Project of the Year, Art Stable
The Wallpaper* 150, Tom Kundig
Washington Aggregates & Concrete Association, Excellence in Concrete Construction, The Pierre
Washington NAIOP Market Adaptation of the Year, Stadium Nissan of Seattle

2010

AIA National Honor Award, Architecture, Outpost
AIA Seattle Honor Award, Citation, Art Stable Hinge
AIA Seattle Honor Award, Citation, T Bailey Offices
Fallingwater Cabin Design Competition, finalist
Fast Company, Top 10 Most Innovative Companies in Architecture, Olson Kundig Architects
IIDA Northern Pacific Chapter INaward, Design IN Hospitality, Winner in Class, Mistral Kitchen
IIDA Northern Pacific Chapter INaward, Design IN Mass, Honorable Mention, Touchstone Offices
Residential Architect Design Award, Merit Award, Gulf Island Cabin
Residential Architect Design Award, Merit Award, Montecito Residence
Seattle magazine, Best of the Decade: Cityscape, Olson Kundig Architects
World Architecture News, House of the Year, The Pierre

2009

AIA Architecture Firm Award, Olson Sundberg Kundig Allen Architects
AIA National Housing Award, Montecito Residence
AIA National Housing Award, Outpost
AIA Northwest and Pacific Region Design Award, Honor Award, Rolling Huts

AIA Northwest and Pacific Region Design
Award, Merit Award, Tye River Cabin
Architectural Record, House of the Month,
Montecito Residence
Chicago Athenaeum, American Architecture
Award, Outpost
Chicago Athenaeum, American Architecture
Award, Rolling Huts
Residential Architect Design Award, Grand
Award: Custom Home, Outpost
Residential Architect Design Award, Grand
Award: Outbuilding, Rolling Huts
Sunset-AIA Western Home Award, Custom
Home, Honorable Mention, Montecito
Residence
TreeHugger, Best of Green: Design +
Architecture, Best Architect, Tom
Kundig, Olson Sundberg Kundig Allen
Architects

2008
AIA National Honor Award, Architecture,
Delta Shelter
AIA Northwest and Pacific Region Design
Award, Honor Award, Montecito
Residence
AIA Northwest and Pacific Region Design
Award, Merit Award, Outpost
Architectural Record, Record House,
Rolling Huts
Chicago Athenaeum, American Architecture
Award, Montecito Residence
Cooper Hewitt, Smithsonian Design
Museum, National Design Award,
Architecture Design Award, Tom Kundig
Northwest Design Awards, Montecito
Residence

2007
AIA National Housing Award, Delta Shelter
AIA National Housing Award, Tye River
Cabin
AIA Northwest and Pacific Region Design
Award, Honor Award, Delta Shelter
AIA Seattle Honor Award, Commendation,
Montecito Residence
AIA Seattle Merit Award, Outpost
AIA Seattle Merit Award, Rolling Huts
American Academy of Arts and Letters,
Academy Award in Architecture,
Tom Kundig
Chicago Athenaeum, American Architecture
Award, Delta Shelter
Chicago Athenaeum, American Architecture
Award, Tye River Cabin
Residential Architect Design Award, Grand
Award, Artist's Studio

2006
AIA Seattle Merit Award, Delta Shelter
AIA Seattle Merit Award, Tye River Cabin
Architectural Record, Record House,
Delta Shelter
IIDA Northern Pacific Chapter INaward,
Design IN Home, Honorable Mention,
Artist's Studio
The MacDowell Colony, fellowship, winter/
spring 2006
Residential Architect Design Award, Grand
Award, Delta Shelter
Seattle Homes & Lifestyles magazine,
Seattle 100: The People, Places & Things
That Define Seattle Design, Olson
Sundberg Kundig Allen Architects

2005
Cooper Hewitt, Smithsonian Design
Museum, National Design Award,
Architecture Design Award finalist,
Tom Kundig
IIDA Northern Pacific Chapter INaward,
Olson Kundig Architects Office
Metropolitan Home Design 100, North
Seattle Residence
Residential Architect Design Award, Grand
Award, Chicken Point Cabin

2004
AIA College of Fellows, Tom Kundig
AIA National Honor Award, The Brain
AIA National Honor Award, Chicken
Point Cabin
Architectural League of New York, Emerging
Voice, Tom Kundig
Chicago Athenaeum, American Architecture
Award, Chicken Point Cabin
Masonry Institute of Washington,
Residential Honor Award, Lake House

2003
AIA Northwest and Pacific Region
Design Award, Honor Award,
Chicken Point Cabin

2002
AIA Seattle Honor Award, Chicken
Point Cabin

2001
AIA Northwest and Pacific Region Design
Award, Honor Award, The Brain

2000
AIA Seattle Honor Award, The Brain
AIA Summit Western International Design
Award, Merit Award, Studio House

1999
AIA National Honor Award (associate to
Steven Holl Architects), Chapel of
St. Ignatius
AIA Seattle Conceptual Honor Award,
The Brain

1998
AIA National Design Award (associate to
Steven Holl Architects), Chapel of
St. Ignatius
AIA Northwest and Pacific Region Design
Award, Honor Award, Studio House

1997
AIA National Religious Architecture Award
(associate to Steven Holl Architects),
Chapel of St. Ignatius
AIA Northwest and Pacific Region Design
Award, Honor Award, City House
AIA Seattle Merit Award, Studio House

1996
AIA Seattle Conceptual Citation Award,
Home House
AIA Seattle Honor Award, Citation,
City House

1994
AIA Northwest and Pacific Region Design
Award, Merit Award, Meadow House

1993
AIA Seattle Honor Award, Commendation,
Meadow House

1981
Blueprint Award, Seattle Art Museum

Selected Teaching & Lectures

2018
AIA National Convention, "Cocktails and
Conversations," panelist
Rural Studio commencement speaker

2017
AIA New York, "Cocktails and
Conversations," panelist
Construction Specifications Institute
ProSpec, speaker
Dallas Architecture Forum, "Design
Symposium: Material Design," panelist

2016
AIA Charleston + CAC.C Lecture Series,
"Tom Kundig: Works," lecturer

Royal College of Art, "The Rise of the Maker
Architect: From Hot-Rodding to
Resilience," keynote speaker

2015
AIA Louisiana, "Celebrate Architecture—
Baton Rouge," panelist
AIA National Conference, "Urban Sketching,"
panelist
The Barnes Museum, lecturer
Dallas Architectural Forum, lecturer
Hallstatt Technical College, lecturer
Texas Society of Architects, Design
Conference, "Craft," lecturer
University of Southern California, School
of Architecture, Jon Adams Jerde,
FAIA Chair in Architecture and
visiting professor
University of Texas at Arlington, School of
Architecture, lecturer

2014
Iowa State University, Herbert Lecture in
Architecture, keynote speaker
Nevada Museum of Art, "DICE 2014: CRAFT,"
lecturer
Los Altos Neutra House, Architecture and
Design Series, keynote speaker
Tulane School of Architecture, lecturer

2013
AIA Western Mountain Region Conference,
"Landscape, Community, Craft,"
keynote speaker
Alaska Design Forum, "HERE: From Global
to Hyper Local," lecturer
Northwest Museum of Arts and Culture, AIA
Spokane Visiting Lecture Series, lecturer
The Project Room, "Successful People
Talking about Failure," lecturer
Stanford University, "Architecture &
Landscape," lecturer
Starbucks Headquarters, Global Design
Innovation Summit, lecturer
University of Southern California, School of
Architecture, Jon Adams Jerde, FAIA
Chair in Architecture, keynote speaker

2012
Cement Concrete & Aggregates Australia,
"C+A TALKS," lecturer

2011
Arizona State University, visiting
design critic
Ghost 13 International Architecture
Conference, "Tom Kundig: Craft/Context/
Hot Rodding," lecturer

Royal Academy of Arts, London, "Landscape, Community and Craft," lecturer
University of Washington, College of Built Environments, "Landscape, Community and Craft," lecturer

2010
North Carolina State University School of Architecture/AIA Triangle Chapter Joint Lecture Series, "Sfd Place," lecturer
San Antonio AIA, lecture series, lecturer
University of Arkansas, Fay Jones School of Architecture, John G. Williams Distinguished Professor
University of Arkansas, Fay Jones School of Architecture, lecturer
University of Texas, Austin, School of Architecture, lecturer

2009
Architalx lecture series, Portland, Maine, lecturer
Arts Council of Sonoma County, North x North Coast lecture series, lecturer
The Back Room Lectures, Portland, Oregon, panelist
National Building Museum, Spotlight on Design, lecturer
Seattle Art Museum and Cascade Land Conservancy, "Art, Design & Sustainability: A Dialogue," panelist
Street of Eames, Portland, Oregon, lecturer
University of Washington, College of Built Environments, Dean's Distinguished Lecture, lecturer

2008
University of Arizona, College of Architecture and Landscape Architecture, lecturer
Washington University in St. Louis, Sam Fox School of Design & Visual Arts, lecturer

2007
Arizona State University, College of Architecture, lecturer
Oklahoma State University, College of Architecture, lecturer
University of Florida, College of Architecture, lecturer

2006
AIA National Convention, "Architects Discuss America's New Regionalism," panelist
AIA National Convention, "Opening Details: Accessible Transition between Inside and Out," panelist
Residential Architect, Reinvention conference, keynote speaker
Syracuse University, College of Architecture, D. Kenneth Sargent Visiting Design Critic
University of Illinois at Urbana-Champaign, School of Architecture, lecturer
University of Washington, College of Architecture and Urban Planning, lecturer

2005
AIA Louisiana, "Celebrate Architecture—Baton Rouge," panelist
American Federation of the Arts, "Restructure: New Form in Architectural Mesh," lecturer
Cooper Hewitt, Smithsonian Design Museum, lecturer
Sun Valley Center for the Arts, lecturer
University of Washington, College of Architecture and Urban Planning, "New Wave of Structural Engineering in Architecture," panelist
Western Interiors & Design Conference, Los Angeles, California, lecturer

2004
AIA Seattle, "Fellows Series: Tom Kundig, FAIA," lecturer
Architectural League of New York, "Emerging Architect," lecturer
National Building Museum, "Liquid Stone Exhibit," lecturer
Portland State University, College of Architecture, "Tom Kundig: Work," lecturer
Texas Tech University, College of Architecture, visiting design critic
University of Oregon, Department of Landscape Architecture, visiting instructor in Kyoto, Japan
Winston Wachter Gallery, "The Intersection between Art, Design & Architecture," panelist

2003
AIA New York City & Bulthaup Lecture Series, "Designing around an Art Collection," lecturer
Art Basel/Miami Beach, "Architecture for Art: Collecting, Conserving and Exhibiting," moderator
Harvard University GSD Seminar, lecturer
Western Interiors Design Conference, Cody, Wyoming, lecturer

2002
AIA Northwest & Pacific Region Conference, panelist

2001
Architectural Institute of British Columbia, lecturer
University of Oregon, visiting design critic in Kyoto, Japan

2000
University of Oregon Architectural Lecture Series, lecturer

1999
University of Washington, graduate design studio, instructor
Washington State University, Department of Architecture, visiting design critic

1997
Pilchuck Glass School, lecturer
Spokane Art School, lecturer

Selected Exhibitions

2017
Vancouver Art Gallery, *Cabin Fever*, including Delta Shelter

2014
KANEKO, *Olson Kundig Anthology*

2013
Portland Museum of Art, *Voices of Design: 25 Years of Architalx*

2012
Royal Scottish Academy, including the Artist's Studio

2011
Louisiana Museum of Modern Art, *Living: Frontiers of Architecture II–IV*

2010
TOTO Gallery MA, Tokyo, *Global Ends: Towards a New Beginning*

2009
Cooper Hewitt, Smithsonian Design Museum, *Design USA: Contemporary Innovation*

2006
Seattle Architecture Foundation, *Ideas in Form 9*
Syracuse University, College of Architecture, *Tom Kundig*

2005
American Foundation of Arts, *Restructure: New Forms in Architectural Mesh*
Seattle Architecture Foundation, *Ideas in Form 8*

2004
National Building Museum, *Liquid Stone: New Architecture in Concrete*
University of Washington, Department of Architecture, *Selected Work: 1997–Now*
Washington State University, Department of Architecture, *Selected Work: 1997–Now*

2001
Architectural Institute of British Columbia, wineries exhibition, Mission Hill Winery
Kelowna Art Museum, Mission Hill Winery

1998
University of Washington, Process House
Washington State University, *Tom Kundig: Work*

1997
Spokane Arts School, *Process House*

Project Credits

9th & Thomas

Completed: 2019
Location: Seattle, Washington
Team: Tom Kundig, FAIA, RIBA, design principal; Kirsten R. Murray, FAIA, principal; Jeff Ocampo, LEED AP, project manager; John Hallock, LEED AP, project architect; Sasha Leon, Hayden Robinson, Brian Walters, LEED AP, Jamie Slagel, and Bryan Berkas, architectural staff; Naomi Mason, IIDA, LEED AP, Laina Navarro, and Irina Bokova, lobby interior design; Phil Turner, gizmo design
Consultants: Architectural Elements (custom stair fabricator); Magnusson Klemencic Associates (civil and structural engineer); McKinstry (mechanical, electrical, and plumbing engineer); Resolute (lighting design and custom lighting fabricator); SiteWorkshop (landscape architect); Turner Exhibits (custom exterior kinetic screen fabricator)
Contractor: Sellen Construction

9th & Thomas Residence

Completed: 2019
Location: Seattle, Washington
Team: Tom Kundig, FAIA, RIBA, design principal; Kirsten R. Murray, FAIA, principal; Jeff Ocampo, LEED AP, project manager; Jamie Slagel, project architect; John Hallock, LEED AP, and Sasha Leon, architectural staff; Phil Turner, gizmo design
Interiors: Stefan Design Studio
Consultants: Architectural Elements (gizmo and casework fabricator); Magnusson Klemencic Associates (civil and structural engineer); McKinstry (mechanical, electrical, and plumbing engineer and lighting design); SiteWorkshop (landscape architect)
Contractor: Sellen Construction

100 Stewart Hotel & Apartments

Completed: 2016
Location: Seattle, Washington
Team: Tom Kundig, FAIA, RIBA, design principal; Kirsten R. Murray, FAIA, principal; Jeff Ocampo, LEED AP, project manager; Brian Walters, LEED AP, project architect; Hayden Robinson, Edward Lalonde, Evan Harlan, and Lori Kirsis, architectural staff
Interiors: Jensen Fey Architects
Consultants: Allegion (door hardware specifications); Associated Earth Sciences (geotechnical); BRC Acoustics & Audiovisual Design (acoustical engineer); Bush, Roed & Hitchings (surveyor); Friday Group (specifications); Glumac (mechanical design assist engineer); Hawk Mechanical (plumbing engineer); Holaday-Parks (mechanical engineer and energy analysis consultant); Holmes Electric (electrical engineer); Lerch Bates (elevator); Magnusson Klemencic Associates (civil and structural engineer); RDH Building Science (building envelope); Swift Company (landscape architect)
Contractor: Turner Construction

Bilgola Beach House

Completed: 2018
Location: Sydney, Australia
Team: Tom Kundig, FAIA, RIBA, design principal; Kevin Kudo-King, AIA, LEED AP, principal; Simon Clews, project manager and project architect; Motomi Kudo-King, Lindsay Kunz, and Martina Bendel, architectural staff; Debbie Kennedy, LEED AP ID+C, interior design; Megan Adams, Casey Hill, and Maresa Patterson, interior design staff
Interiors: Olson Kundig
Consultants: Advanced Design Innovations (gizmo fabrication); Auric Projects (client representative); BBF Planners (planner); CAB Consulting (landscape architect); Horton Coastal Engineering (coastal engineer); JK Geotechnics (geotech consultant); KB Architectural Services with Phil Turner (gizmo design); Niteo Lighting (lighting design); Partridge Engineering (civil and structural engineer); RJ Air (mechanical engineer); TILT Industrial Design (gizmo fabrication)
Contractor: Bellevarde Constructions

The Bo Bartlett Center

Completed: 2017
Location: Columbus, Georgia
Team: Tom Kundig, FAIA, RIBA, design principal; Edward Lalonde, project manager; Angus MacGregor, RIBA, LEED AP BD+C, project manager; Gus Lynch, LEED AP, project architect; Nate Boyd and Ryan Patterson, architectural staff; Phil Turner, gizmo design
Associate Architect: Hecht Burdeshaw Architects
Consultants: Applied Building Information (specifications); Lighting Designs (lighting design); Midsouth Steel (gizmo fabrication); NBP Engineers (mechanical and electrical engineer); Wright Engineering (structural engineer)
Contractor: JE Dunn Construction

Burke Museum of Natural History and Culture

Completion: 2019
Location: Seattle, Washington
Team: Tom Kundig, FAIA, RIBA, design principal; Stephen Yamada-Heidner, AIA, LEED AP, principal and project manager; Edward Lalonde and Justin Helmbrecht, LEED AP, project architects; Gavin Argo, Julia Khorsand, and Olivier Landa, AIA, LEED AP BD+C, architectural staff; Phil Turner, gizmo design; Margaret Undine, interior design staff
Consultants: BergerABAM (laboratories); Cite Specific (specifications); GGN (landscape architect); Karen Braitmayer (accessibility consultant); Lerch Bates (elevators); Magnusson Klemencic Associates (civil and structural engineer); Niteo Lighting (lighting design); RDH (building envelope); Stantec (electrical engineer); Turner Exhibits (gizmo fabrication); Walter Crimm Associates (museum programmer); WSP (mechanical engineer)
Contractor: Skanska

Charles Smith Wines Jet City

Completed: 2015
Location: Seattle, Washington
Team: Tom Kundig, FAIA, RIBA, design principal; Mark Olthoff, AIA, LEED AP, project manager; Debbie Kennedy, LEED AP ID+C, interior design
Interiors: Olson Kundig
Consultants: Madden & Baughman Engineering (structural engineer); PCS Structural Solutions (structural engineer); Thomas Kinsman (civil engineer); Warner Mechanical Engineering (mechanical engineer)
Contractor: Foushée & Associates

CheckMate Winery Pop-Up

Completed: 2017
Location: Oliver, British Columbia
Team: Tom Kundig, FAIA, RIBA, design principal; Edward Lalonde, principal; Laura Bartunek, project manager and project architect; Phil Turner, gizmo design
Consultants: Meiklejohn Architects (BC collaborating architect); Pentagon Engineering Ltd. (structural engineer)
Contractor: Wildstone Construction

Chemin Byron

Completed: 2017
Location: Geneva, Switzerland
Team: Tom Kundig, FAIA, RIBA, design principal; Steven Rainville, AIA, LEED AP, project architect and project manager; Katherine Ranieri and Sini Kamppari Pearson, architectural staff; Debbie Kennedy, LEED AP ID+C, interior design
Associate Architect: Nocea Architecture
Interiors: Olson Kundig
Consultants: Nocea Architecture (civil engineer); O- Lighting (lighting design); Thomas Jundt Ingénieurs Civils (structural engineer)
Contractor: Nocea Architecture

Collywood

Completed: 2018
Location: West Hollywood, California, United States
Team: Tom Kundig, FAIA, RIBA, design principal; Elizabeth Bianchi Conklin, AIA, LEED AP, project manager; Patricia Flores, Cameron Shampine, and Evan Harlan, architectural staff; Debbie Kennedy, LEED AP ID+C, interior design; Amanda Chenoweth and Ana Brainard, interior design staff
Interiors: Olson Kundig
Consultants: Black's Electric (audiovisual consultant); Buratti & Associates (electrical engineer); Clark & White Landscape (landscape architect); Crest Real Estate (land use consultant); Holden Water (pool and hot tub design); Illum Lighting Design (lighting design); KB Architectural Services with Phil Turner (gizmo design); Lee Gilman Builders (owner's representative); Meta Design (gizmo fabrication); Newton

Energy (energy consultant); PCS Structural (structural engineer); Prime Aire (mechanical engineer); T Engineering Group (civil engineer)

Contractor: MG Partners

Comedor Restaurant

Completed: 2019
Location: Austin, Texas
Team: Tom Kundig, FAIA, RIBA, design principal; Bob Jakubik, AIA, LEED AP, project manager; Joe Fillipelli and Claire Fontaine, architectural staff; Laina Navarro, interior design; Megan Adams, interior design staff; Phil Turner, gizmo design
Associate Architect: McKinney/York Architects
Interiors: Olson Kundig
Consultants: Aptus Engineering (mechanical, electrical, and plumbing engineer); Drophouse Design (gizmo fabrication); KB Architectural Services with Phil Turner (gizmo design); Micki Spencer (interior production); O- Lighting (lighting design); Stantec (civil engineer); Structures (structural engineer); The Garden Design Studio (landscape architect)
Contractor: The Burt Group

Costa Rica Treehouse

Completed: 2017
Location: Santa Teresa, Costa Rica
Team: Tom Kundig, FAIA, RIBA, design principal; Kevin Kudo-King, AIA, LEED AP, principal; Martina Bendel, project architect
Associate Architect: Daniel Sancho
Consultants: Daniel Sancho (structural engineer); Energetica Soluciones y Consultoria (mechanical and electrical engineer); KB Architectural Services (gizmo design); Niteo Lighting (lighting design); Vida Design Studio (landscape architect)
Contractor: Dante Medri

Dallas Apartment

Completed: 2016
Location: Dallas, Texas
Team: Tom Kundig, FAIA, RIBA, design principal; Megan Zimmerman, LEED AP BD+C, project architect; Laina Navarro, interior design
Interiors: Emily Summers Design Associates
Consultants: Blum Consulting Engineers (mechanical, electrical, and plumbing engineer); Facility Performance Associates (energy inspector); Gromatzky Dupree & Associates (shell / core architect); Inspec (Dallas Green Building Code consultant); KB Architectural Services (gizmo design); L.A. Fuess Partners (structural engineer); Sparling/Stantec (acoustical engineer); Studio Lumina (lighting design)
Contractor: Construction Zone

Dragonfly

Completed: 2016
Location: Whitefish, Montana
Team: Tom Kundig, FAIA, RIBA, design principal; Justin Helmbrecht, LEED AP, project architect; Ellen Cecil, project manager; Debbie Kennedy, LEED AP ID+C, interior design; Laina Navarro, Brianna Schoeneman, and Irina Bokova, interior design staff; Phil Turner, gizmo design
Interiors: Olson Kundig
Consultants: Acutech (gizmo fabrication); KB Architectural Services with Phil Turner (gizmo design); MCE Structural Consultants (structural engineer); O- Lighting (lighting design); White Cloud Design (landscape architect)
Contractor: Bear Mountain Builders

Hale Lana

Completed: 2018
Location: Kona, Hawaii
Team: Tom Kundig, FAIA, RIBA, design principal; Todd Matthes, project manager; Katherine Ranieri, project architect; Gregory Nakata, architectural staff; Debbie Kennedy, LEED AP ID+C, interior design; Amanda Chenoweth, Kathy Hanway, Maresa Patterson, and Crisanna Siegert, interior design staff
Interiors: Olson Kundig
Consultants: David Y. Tamura Associates (landscape architect); John K. Maute, PE (photovoltaic consultant); Kai Pono Builders (pool consultant); Kona Wai Engineering (civil engineer); MCE Structural Consultants (structural engineer); Niteo Lighting (lighting design); Spearhead (steel and timber fabrication consultant); WSP (mechanical and electrical engineer)
Contractor: Schuchart/Dow

The Lab

Completed: 2015
Location: Bellevue, Washington, United States
Team: Tom Kundig, FAIA, RIBA, design principal; Ming-Lee Yuan, AIA, project manager and project architect; Eric Druse, LEED AP, architectural staff; Phil Turner, gizmo design
Consultants: DCI (civil and structural engineer); Foy Group (electrical engineer); Johansen Mechanical (mechanical engineer); Niteo Lighting (lighting design)
Contractor: Schuchart

Martin's Lane Winery

Completed: 2016
Location: Kelowna, British Columbia
Team: Tom Kundig, FAIA, RIBA, design principal; Steve Grim, AIA, LEED AP BD+C, project manager
Consultants: CTQ (civil engineer); Falcon Engineering (electrical engineer); GCA Architects (interior architecture); Glotman Simpson Consulting Engineers (structural engineer); Laurence Ferar (winery design consultant); Meiklejohn Architects (BC collaborating architect); Niteo Lighting (lighting design); Paul Sangha Landscape Architecture (landscape architect); Rocky Point Engineering (mechanical engineer)
Contractor: PCL Construction

Maxon House

Completed: 2016
Location: Carnation, Washington,
Team: Tom Kundig, FAIA, RIBA, design principal; Edward Lalonde, project manager and project architect; Phil Turner, gizmo design
Consultants: Lighting Designs (lighting design); MCE Structural Consultants (structural engineer); Turner Exhibits (gizmo engineering)
Contractor: Schuchart/Dow

Meg Home

Completed: 2016
Location: Seattle, Washington
Team: Tom Kundig, FAIA, RIBA, design principal; Angus MacGregor, RIBA, LEED AP BD+C, project manager; Justin Helmbrecht, LEED AP, and Hayden Robinson, project architects; Debbie Kennedy, LEED AP ID+C, interior design; Ana Brainard, interior design staff; Phil Turner, gizmo design
Interiors: Olson Kundig
Consultants: Alpine Welding (gizmo fabrication); Coughlin Porter Lundeen (civil engineer); KB Architectural Services with Phil Turner (gizmo design); MCE Structural Consultants (structural engineer); Ohashi Landscape Services (landscape architect); O- Lighting (lighting design)
Contractor: Schuchart/Dow

Millerton Farmhouse

Completed: 2016
Location: Millerton, New York
Team: Tom Kundig, FAIA, RIBA, design principal; Mark Olthoff, AIA, LEED AP, project manager; Dawn McConaghy, AIA, LEED AP BD+C, project architect; Matthew Hostetler, LEED AP, architectural staff; Debbie Kennedy, LEED AP ID+C, interior design; Ana Brainard, interior design staff; Phil Turner, gizmo design
Interiors: Olson Kundig
Consultants: Berlinghoff Electrical Contracting (electrical engineer); Devore Associates (landscape architect); Old Farm Nursery (plant selection and installation); Renfro Design Group (lighting design); Rennia Engineering Design (civil engineer); Silman (structural engineer); William Perotti & Sons (mechanical engineer)
Contractor: United Construction & Engineering

MrSteam

Completed: 2018
Location: Long Island City, New York,
Team: Tom Kundig, FAIA, RIBA, design principal; Jamie Slagel, principal / project manager

Consultant: Innovative Engineering Services (mechanical and electrical engineer)
Contractor: MUECKE

Rio House

Completed: 2018
Location: Rio de Janeiro, Brazil
Team: Tom Kundig, FAIA, RIBA, design principal; Edward Lalonde, project manager / project architect; Fergus Knox, architectural staff; Phil Turner, gizmo design
Consultants: 12th Avenue Iron (gizmo fabricator); Eleve (steelwork); Front (facade consultant); Isabel Duprat Landscape Architecture (landscape architect); Jose Luiz Canal (project manager / owner's representative); KB Architectural Services with Phil Turner (gizmo design); MCE Structural Consultants and Mauro Jorge (structural engineers); O- Lighting Design (lighting design); WSP and GreenWatt (mechanical, electrical, and plumbing engineers)
Contractor: Construtora São Bento

River House

Completed: 2017
Location: Ketchum, Idaho
Team: Tom Kundig, FAIA, RIBA, design principal; Elizabeth Bianchi Conklin, AIA, LEED AP, project manager; Cameron Shampine, architectural staff; Phil Turner, gizmo design
Consultants: 12th Avenue Iron (metal stair railing fabrication); Eggers Associates (landscape architect); Galena Engineering (civil engineer); JG Works (gizmo fabrication); John Reuter Greenworks (energy consultant); KB Architectural Services with Phil Turner (gizmo design); MCE Structural Consultants (structural engineer); Niteo Lighting (lighting design); Sawtooth Environmental (wetlands consultant)
Contractor: Lee Gilman Builders

Shinsegae International

Completed: 2015
Location: Seoul, South Korea
Team: Tom Kundig, FAIA, RIBA, design principal; Dan Wilson, AIA, managing principal; Jason Roseler, LEED AP, project

architect; Jerry Garcia, LEED AP, Angus MacGregor, RIBA, LEED AP BD+C, Evan Harlan, and Nathan Boyd, architectural staff; Debbie Kennedy, LEED AP ID+C, interior design; Phil Turner, gizmo design
Associate Architect: JUNGLIM Architecture
Consultants: Allworth Design (landscape architecture); CDC (curtain wall / facade design during schematic design phase); Dajung Metal Fabrics Co. (operable and fixed metal mesh panels); Front (curtain wall / facade design during design development, construction documents); Lerch Bates (facade access during schematic design phase); Magnusson Klemencic Associates (structural engineer); Tino Kwan Lighting Consultants (lighting design); WSP (mechanical engineer)
Contractor: Shinsegae Engineering and Construction

Teton House

Completed: 2018
Location: Jackson Hole, Wyoming
Team: Tom Kundig, FAIA, RIBA, design principal; Steve Grim, LEED AP BD+C, project manager; Ryan Patterson, architectural staff; Christine Burkland, interior design; Nikole Hester, interior design staff; Phil Turner, gizmo design
Interiors: Olson Kundig
Consultants: Agrostis (landscape architect); Jorgensen (civil engineer); KB Architectural Services with Phil Turner (gizmo design); KL&A (structural engineer); Turner Exhibits (gizmo fabrication); WSP (mechanical engineer)
Contractor: Tim Reiser

Tillamook Creamery Visitor Center

Completed: 2018
Location: Tillamook, Oregon
Team: Tom Kundig, FAIA, RIBA, design principal, architecture; Alan Maskin, design principal, exhibits; Marlene Chen, AIA, LEED AP, project manager; Ming-Lee Yuan, AIA, project architect; Michelle Arab, ASLA, landscape architect; Laina Navarro, interior design; Daniel Renner, Jerome Tryon, and Nathan Petty, architectural staff; Juan Ferreira, architectural staff, exhibits; ChiaLin Ma, landscape architecture staff; Francesca Krisli, interior design staff

Interiors: Olson Kundig
Consultants: BRC Acoustics (acoustical engineer); CEI (mechanical engineer); CIDA (structural engineer); Code Unlimited (code consultant); Cundiff Engineering (electrical engineer); Formations (exhibit fabricator); GHD (civil engineer); Karen Braitmayer (accessibility consultant); Lovett Design and Owen Davey (illustrators); Niteo Lighting (lighting design); Rand Associates and Ellipse Studio (content development / writing); Studio SC (graphic design); The Friday Group (specifications)
Contractor: Precision Construction

Triptych

Completed: 2017
Location: Yarrow Point, Washington
Team: Tom Kundig, FAIA, RIBA, design principal; Ming-Lee Yuan, AIA, project manager; Eric Druse, LEED AP, project architect; Mark Wettstone and Michelle Coetzee, architectural staff; Phil Turner, gizmo design
Interiors: Atelier AM
Consultants: Coughlin Porter Lundeen (civil engineer); GGN (landscape architect); KB Architectural Services with Phil Turner (gizmo design); MCE Structural Consultants (structural engineer); Niteo Lighting (lighting design); WSP (mechanical engineer)
Contractor: Schuchart/Dow

Wagner Education Center, the Center for Wooden Boats

Completed: 2019
Location: Seattle, Washington
Team: Tom Kundig, FAIA, RIBA, design principal; Steven Rainville, AIA, LEED AP, principal; Angus MacGregor, RIBA, LEED AP BD+C, project architect; Derek Santo, Dawn McConaghy, and Simon Clews, architectural staff; Vikram Sami, AIA, BEMP, LEED AP, building performance; Tom Kundig, Alan Maskin, and Angus MacGregor, hanging boat installation, exhibition design; Phil Turner, gizmo design
Consultants: Adapt Engineering (geotech consultant); Alpine Welding (gizmo fabrication); Karen Braitmayer (accessibility consultant); KB

Architectural Services with Phil Turner (gizmo design); KPFF (civil and structural engineer); RDH (building envelope); Stantec (electrical engineer, lighting design, and acoustic consultant); WSP (mechanical engineer)
Contractor: Schuchart

Wasatch House

Completed: 2016
Location: Salt Lake City, Utah
Team: Tom Kundig, FAIA, RIBA, design principal; Ming-Lee Yuan, AIA, project architect; Kozo Nozawa, Mark Wettstone, Jordan Leppert, Megan Quinn, and Paul Schlachter, architectural staff; Laina Navarro, interior design; Irina Bokova, interior design staff; Phil Turner, gizmo design
Interiors: Olson Kundig
Consultants: Gordon Geotechnical Engineering (geotechnical consultant); HELIUS Lighting (lighting design); LOCI (landscape architect); MCE Structural Consultants (structural engineer); Nielson Engineering (mechanical and electrical engineer); Spearhead (timber fabrication consultant); Stantec (civil engineer)
Contractor: Edge Builders

West Edge Tower

Completed: 2018
Location: Seattle, Washington
Team: Tom Kundig, FAIA, RIBA, design principal; Kirsten R. Murray, FAIA, principal; Jerry Garcia, LEED AP, project manager; Thomas Brown, LEED AP, Nathan Boyd, Evan Harlan, Edward Lalonde, Daniel Ralls, and Christopher Gerrick, AIA, LEED AP BD+C, architectural staff
Associate Architect: Ankrom Moisan Architecture
Consultants: Hart Crowser (geotechnical engineer); Holmes Electric (electrical engineer); McKinstry (mechanical engineer); MKA (civil and structural engineer); Rushing (lighting design); Site Workshop (landscape architect); Sparling (acoustical engineer)
Contractor: Sellen Construction

Tom Kundig, FAIA, RIBA, is a principal and owner of Olson Kundig. Over the past three decades he has received some of the world's highest design honors, including a National Design Award for architecture design from the Cooper Hewitt, Smithsonian Design Museum and an Academy Award in Architecture from the American Academy of Arts and Letters. In 2016 he was elected to the National Academy of Design as a National Academician in Architecture, and in 2018 he received the American Institute of Architects (AIA) Seattle chapter's Gold Medal, the highest honor that AIA Seattle can confer on one of its members.

In addition to receiving scores of design awards—including ten National Honor Awards, ten National Housing Awards, and a Committee on the Environment Top Ten Award, all from the AIA—Kundig's work has appeared in thousands of publications worldwide and on the covers of the *New York Times Magazine*, *Architect*, *Architectural Record*, *Architectural Digest*, and *The Plan*. Kundig's Shinsegae International received the World Architecture News Tall Buildings Award in 2017, and his Meg Home, Rolling Huts, and Delta Shelter projects have all received Record House awards. The Pierre was named the World Architecture News House of the Year in 2010. His work can be found on five continents, in locations ranging from Costa Rica to Brazil, New Zealand, China, Mexico, Sweden, and Austria. Kundig regularly lectures and serves on design juries around the world, and he was named in the Wallpaper* 150 as a key individual who has influenced, inspired, and improved the way we live, work, and travel. Under his leadership Olson Kundig has received an AIA National Architecture Firm Award, has been included in the AD100 list for more than ten years, and for three years has been named one of the Top Ten Most Innovative Companies in Architecture by *Fast Company*.

Published by
Princeton Architectural Press
202 Warren Street
Hudson, New York 12534
www.papress.com

Editor: Sara Stemen
Designers: Miko McGinty, Rebecca Sylvers, and Claire Bidwell

Library of Congress Cataloging-in-Publication Data
Names: Kundig, Tom, author. | Rozzo, Mark, writer of foreword. |
    Chaiken, Michael, interviewer.
Title: Tom Kundig : working title / Tom Kundig.
Description: First edition. | Hudson, New York : Princeton Architectural
    Press, [2020] | Summary: "An international assortment of houses and
    large-scale works from a master of contextually astute, richly detailed
    architecture."— Provided by publisher.
Identifiers: LCCN 2019036815 (print) | LCCN 2019036816 (ebook) |
    ISBN 9781616898991 (hardcover) | ISBN 9781616898991 (epub)
Subjects: LCSH: Kundig, Tom—Themes, motives.
Classification: LCC NA737.K86 A4 2020 (print) | LCC NA737.K86 (ebook) |
    DDC 728—dc23
LC record available at https://lccn.loc.gov/2019036815
LC ebook record available at https://lccn.loc.gov/2019036816

Image Credits
Maíra Acayaba: 269–79
Mikel Amias / Olson Kundig: 28 (bottom), 72–73, 77, 176–79, 252–54
Richard Barnes: 344–45
Gabe Border: 170–71
Nicholas Calcott: 18–19, 88–95
Ken Dundas: 16
Noah Forbes: 354
Nic Lehoux: 7–9, 11 (bottom), 13, 32–33, 36–42, 44, 46, 52, 55–59, 64, 65 (top),
    66–69, 71, 75–76, 78–87, 96–97, 100–101, 103–37, 140–53, 156–63,
    165–69, 182–91, 193–94, 196–207, 209–14, 237, 240–42, 244–45,
    261–63, 265–67, 298–309, 321–29, 331–43, 347, 352–53
Aaron Leitz: 26–27, 28 (top), 49–51, 53–54, 60–61 (top), 98–99,
    102, 173–75, 180–81, 215–19, 238–39, 243, 246–49, 255–59, 293–97,
    312–13, 316, 349
Matthew Millman: 220–29, 231–35, 282–91, 310–11, 314–15, 317–19
James O'Mara: 138–39
Ryan Patterson / Olson Kundig: 348
Andrew Pogue: 2
Kevin Scott / Olson Kundig: 45, 47, 62–63, 65 (bottom), 155
Kyungsub Shin: 35
Aaron Straight / Soulcraft Allstars: 350–51
Adam L. Weintraub: 11 (top), 250–51